EPHESIANS

J. Vernon McGee

THOMAS NELSON PUBLISHERS

Nashville

Copyright © 1991 by Thru the Bible Radio

Published in Nashville, Tennessee, by Thomas Nelson, Inc.

Scripture quotations are from the KING JAMES VERSION of the Bible.

Library of Congress Cataloging-in-Publication Data

McGee, J. Vernon (John Vernon), 1904–1988
    [Thru the Bible with J. Vernon McGee]
    Thru the Bible commentary series / J. Vernon McGee.
      p.   cm.
    Reprint. Originally published: Thru the Bible with J. Vernon McGee. 1975.
    Includes bibliographical references.
    ISBN 0-7852-1051-2 (TR)
    ISBN 0-8407-3299-6 NRM
    1. Bible—Commentaries. I. Title.
BS491.2.M37   1991
220.7′7—dc20
                                 90–41340
                                 CIP

Printed in the United States of America
3 4 5 6 7 8 9 — 99 98 97 96 95

CONTENTS

EPHESIANS

Preface v

Introduction vii

Outline xiv

Chapter 1 17

Chapter 2 63

Chapter 3 91

Chapter 4 107

Chapter 5 135

Chapter 6 161

Bibliography 189

PREFACE

The radio broadcasts of the Thru the Bible Radio five-year program were transcribed, edited, and published first in single-volume paperbacks to accommodate the radio audience.

There has been a minimal amount of further editing for this publication. Therefore, these messages are not the word-for-word recording of the taped messages which went out over the air. The changes were necessary to accommodate a reading audience rather than a listening audience.

These are popular messages, prepared originally for a radio audience. They should not be considered a commentary on the entire Bible in any sense of that term. These messages are devoid of any attempt to present a theological or technical commentary on the Bible. Behind these messages is a great deal of research and study in order to interpret the Bible from a popular rather than from a scholarly (and too-often boring) viewpoint.

We have definitely and deliberately attempted "to put the cookies on the bottom shelf so that the kiddies could get them."

The fact that these messages have been translated into many languages for radio braodcasting and have been received with enthusiasm reveals the need for a simple teaching of the whole Bible for the masses of the world.

I am indebted to many people and to many sources for bringing this volume into existence. I should express my especial thanks to my secretary, Gertrude Cutler, who supervised the editorial work; to Dr. Elliott R. Cole, my associate, who handled all the detailed work with the publishers; and finally, to my wife Ruth for tenaciously encouraging me from the beginning to put my notes and messages into printed form.

Solomon wrote, ". . . of making many books there is no end; and much study is a weariness of the flesh" (Eccl. 12:12). On a sea of books that flood the marketplace, we launch this series of THRU THE BIBLE with the hope that it might draw many to the one Book, *The Bible*.

J. VERNON McGEE

The Epistle to the
EPHESIANS

INTRODUCTION

A quartet of men left Rome in the year A.D. 62 bound for the province of Asia which was located in what was designated as Asia Minor and is currently called Turkey. These men had on their persons four of the most sublime compositions of the Christian faith. These precious documents would be invaluable if they were in existence today. Rome did not comprehend the significance of the writings of an unknown prisoner. If she had, these men would have been apprehended and the documents seized.

When these men bade farewell to the apostle Paul, each was given an epistle to bear to his particular constituency. These four letters are in the Word of God, and they are designated the "Prison Epistles of Paul," since he wrote them while he was imprisoned in Rome. He was awaiting a hearing before Nero who was the Caesar at that time. Paul as a Roman citizen had appealed his case to the emperor, and he was waiting to be heard.

This quartet of men and their respective places of abode can be identified:

(1) Epaphroditus was from Philippi, and he had the Epistle to the Philippians (see Phil. 4:18); (2) Tychicus was from Ephesus, and he had the Epistle to the Ephesians (see Eph. 6:21); (3) Epaphras was from Colosse, and he had the Epistle to the Colossians (see Col. 4:12); and (4) Onesimus was a runaway slave from Colosse, and he had the Epistle to Philemon who was his master (see Philem. 10).

These epistles present a composite picture of Christ, the church, the Christian life, and the interrelationship and functioning of them all. These different facets present the Christian life on the highest plane.

Ephesians presents the church which is Christ's body. This is the invisible church of which Christ is the Head.

Colossians presents Christ as the Head of the body, the church. The emphasis is upon Christ rather than on the church. In Ephesians the emphasis is on the body, and in Colossians the emphasis is on the Head.

Philippians presents Christian living with Christ as the dynamic. "I can do all things through Christ which strengtheneth me" (Phil. 4:13).

Philemon presents Christian living in action in a pagan society. Paul wrote to Philemon, who was the master of Onesimus and a Christian: "If thou count me therefore a partner, receive him as myself. If he hath wronged thee, or oweth thee aught, put that on mine account" (Philem. 17–18).

The gospel walked in shoe leather in the first century, and it worked. This is the thing that we are going to see in this Epistle to the Ephesians.

Ephesians reveals the church as God's masterpiece, a mystery not revealed in the Old Testament (see Eph. 2:10). It is more wonderful than any temple made with hands, constructed of living stones, indwelt by the Holy Spirit. It is the body of Christ in the world to walk as He would walk and to wrestle against the wiles of the devil. Someday the church will leave the world and be presented to Christ as a bride.

Dr. Arthur T. Pierson called Ephesians "Paul's third-heaven epistle." Another has called it "the Alps of the New Testament." It is the Mount Whitney of the High Sierras of all Scripture. This is the *church epistle*. Many expositors consider this the highest peak of scriptural truth, the very apex of Bible revelation. That may well be true. Some have even suggested that Ephesians is so profound that none but the very elect (in other words, the chosen few) can understand it. I have always noticed that the folk who say this include themselves in that inner circle. To be candid with you, I do not even pretend to be able to probe or plumb the depths of this epistle nor to ascend to its heights.

This epistle is lofty and it is heady. It is difficult to breathe the rarefied air of this epistle—you will find this to be true when we get into it. We will do the very best we can, with the aid of the Holy Spirit who is our guide, to understand it.

On several occasions I have had the privilege of visiting Turkey, and I have visited the sites of all seven churches of Asia Minor. Ephesus is where I spent the most time. I reveled in the opportunity of visiting Ephesus which was the leading church of the seven churches and was in a great city.

The Holy Spirit would not permit Paul on his second missionary journey to enter the province of Asia where Ephesus was the prominent center: "Now when they had gone throughout Phrygia and the region of Galatia, they were forbidden of the Holy Ghost to preach the word in Asia" (Acts 16:6). The Holy Spirit put up a roadblock and said to Paul, "You can't go down there now." We are not told the reason, but we know God's timing is perfect. He would send him there later. So Paul traveled west into Macedonia—to Philippi, down to Berea, down to Athens, over to Corinth, and then, on the way back, he came by Ephesus. Oh, what a tremendous opportunity he saw there! "And he came to Ephesus, and left them there: but he himself entered into the synagogue, and reasoned with the Jews" (Acts 18:19).

Paul was so favorably impressed by the opportunities for missionary work that he promised to return, which he did on his third missionary journey. He discovered that another missionary by the name of Apollos had been there in the interval between his second and third missionary journeys. Apollos had preached only the baptism of John and not the gospel of grace of our Lord Jesus Christ. At that time Apollos didn't know about the Lord Jesus, but later on he himself became a great preacher of the gospel.

Paul began a far-reaching ministry in Ephesus. For two years he spoke in the school of Tyrannus, and the gospel penetrated into every center of the province of Asia. Evidently it was at this time that the churches addressed in the second and third chapters of Revelation were founded by this ministry of Paul.

It is my firm conviction, after having visited Turkey and seen that area and having read a great deal on the excavations that have been made there, that the greatest ministry the gospel has ever had was in what is today modern Turkey. In that day there were millions of people living there. It was the very heart of the Roman Empire. The culture of Greece was no longer in Greece; it was along this coast, the western coast of Turkey, where Ephesus was the leading city. It was a great cultural center and a great religious center. The climate was pleasing, and it was a wonderful place to visit. The Roman emperors came to this area for a vacation. This is where the gospel had its greatest entrance.

Ephesus was the principal city of Asia Minor and probably of the entire eastern section of the Roman Empire. It was second only to Rome. The city had been founded around 2000 B.C. by the Hittites. It was what we call an oriental city, an Asian city, until about 1000 B.C. when the Greeks entered. There one would find a mixture of east and west. Kipling was wrong as far as Ephesus was concerned. He said, "East is east and West is west and ne'er the twain shall meet," but they did meet in Ephesus.

Over this long period of about twenty-five hundred years, Ephesus was one of the great cities of the world. It was on a harbor that is now all filled up, silted in. It is not a harbor anymore; in fact, it is about six miles from the ocean today. At the time Paul went there, he sailed right up to that beautiful white marble freeway. It was a very wide street, and the marble for it was supplied from the quarries of Mount Prion.

The Temple of Diana in Ephesus was one of the seven wonders of the ancient world. It was the largest Greek temple ever constructed, 418 by 239 feet, four times larger than the Parthenon but very similar to it. It was built over a marsh on an artificial foundation of skins and charcoal so that it was not affected by earthquakes. The art and wealth of the Ephesian citizens contributed to its adornment. It had 127 graceful columns, some of them richly carved and colored. It contained works of art, such as the picture painted by Apelles of Alexander the Great hurling the thunderbolt.

Inside this beautiful temple was the idol of Diana. This was not the beautiful Diana of Greek mythology. It was the oriental, actually the Anatolian, conception of the goddess of fertility. It was not the goddess of the moon, but the goddess of fertility, a vulgar, many-breasted idol of wood. All sorts of gross immorality took place in the shadow of this temple.

A flourishing trade was carried on in the manufacture of silver shrines or models of the temple. These are often referred to by ancient writers. Few strangers seem to have left Ephesus without such a memorial of their visit, and this artistic business brought no small gain to the craftsman.

It was to such a city that Paul came. He went first to the synagogue and spoke boldly for the space of three months. Then he went into the school of Tyrannus and continued there for two years ". . . so that all they which dwelt in Asia heard the word of the Lord Jesus, both Jews and Greeks" (Acts 19:10). This was probably the high water mark in the missionary labors of Paul. He considered Ephesus his great opportunity and stayed there longer than in any other place. The people of Ephesus heard more Bible teaching from Paul than did any other people, which is the reason he could write to them the deep truths contained in this epistle.

Paul wrote to the Corinthians, "But I will tarry at Ephesus until Pentecost. For a great door and effectual is opened unto me, and there are many adversaries" (1 Cor. 16:8–9). Because Paul's preaching was putting the silversmiths out of business, there was great opposition, and as a result there was a riot in the city. Paul was preaching the gospel of the living God and life through Jesus Christ. God marvelously preserved him, which encouraged him to continue (see Acts 19:23–41). Paul loved this church in Ephesus. His last meeting with the Ephesian elders was a tender farewell (see Acts 20:17–38).

A great company of believers turned to Christ. I think the gospel was more effective in this area than in any place and at any time in the history of the world. I believe the Ephesian church was the highest church spiritually. It is an amazing thing to me that there were people living in that pagan city who understood this epistle—Paul wouldn't have written it to them if they couldn't have understood it. Furthermore, in the Book of Revelation we find that Ephesus is the first one of the seven churches of Asia mentioned in a series of churches that gives the entire history of the church. Ephesus was the church at its best, the church at the highest spiritual level.

You and I today cannot conceive the high spiritual level that the Spirit of God had produced in these Ephesian believers. They loved the person of the Lord Jesus and were drawn to Him. I have been a pastor for many years and I love to minister in our churches today. I must confess, however, that we are far from the person of Christ today. We are so enamored with programs, with church work, with an office in the church, that we get farther and farther from the person of Christ. The essential question is how much we love Him. Paul wrote to the Ephesians that Christ loved the church and gave Himself for it. Do we return that love? Do we respond to Him? Can we say, "I love Him because He first loved me"? This letter to the Ephesians ought to bring us very close to Christ.

Two books of the Bible which the critic says cannot be understood are Ephesians and Revelation. Liberalism says that Revelation is just a conglomerate of symbols that no one can decipher. Liberalism also says that Ephesians is so high it is beyond us.

Let me say that the two books of the Bible which can be arranged mathematically and logically are Ephesians and Revelation. There are no books more logical than they are. Years ago I got tired of hearing folk say, "I believe the Bible from cover to cover," when they didn't even know what was between the covers. They were just making a pious statement. If one really believes it is God's Word, he will try to find out what it says. We need to get off this gimmick of methods and how to communicate to the younger generation and how to better organize the church and instead really learn what is in the Book. To help folk learn what the Bible is all about, I wrote a book called *Briefing the Bible* in which I attempted to give a helpful outline of every book in the Bible. As I was doing this, I found that Ephesians and Revelation were the two easiest books in the Bible to outline. Do you know why? Because they are logical. I don't pretend to understand everything that is in these books, but I do say that they are logical and they are easily outlined.

Paul is logical in Ephesians and John is logical in Revelation. John was told to write of the things he had seen, of things that are, and of things that will be. There is a clear threefold division. And the book is arranged according to sevens. You couldn't find anything better than that. The Epistle to the Ephesians is very logical. Of the six chapters, the first three are about the heavenly calling of the church and are doctrinal. The last three are about the earthly conduct of the church which is very practical. You see, the church has a Head. The Head of the church is Christ, and He is in heaven. We are identified with Him. But the feet of the church are down here on earth. Paul won't leave us sitting up there in the heavenlies; he says, "Walk worthy of the vocation wherewith ye are called" (Eph. 4:1). In other words, Christian, it's nice to sit up there in the heavenlies and boast of your position in Christ, but, for goodness' sake, get down out of your high chair and start walking. We need to remember that in Paul's day believers were walking in a pagan society in the Roman world. The first half is doctrinal and the last half is practical, which makes a very logical division in the book. We need both. We are not to live in the first three chapters only. They are wonderful, but the message must get down here where we live, down where the rubber meets the road.

The doctrinal section is also very logical. In chapter 1 the church is a body. In chapter 2 the church is a temple. In chapter 3 the church is a mystery.

When we get to the practical section, we find in chapter 4 that the church is a new man. The church is to exhibit something new in the world: walking through the world as a new man. In chapter 5 the church will be a bride. Don't get the idea that the church is a bride now; the church is not a bride today. Paul wrote in 2 Corinthians 11:2, ". . . for I have espoused you to one husband, that I may present you as a chaste virgin to Christ." In effect he says, "I'm getting you engaged to Christ today, and someday the church will be His bride." In chapter 6 the church is a soldier. A wag who heard me give this outline said to me, "That's interesting. The church will be a bride, you say, and the church is a soldier. In a lot of marriages down here, they get married and then the fighting starts." Well, that is not the way Paul meant it. He was being very practical. The church is a soldier, and there is an enemy to be fought. There is a battle going on in this world. The bugle has sounded. We need to stand for God today.

OUTLINE

I. **Doctrinal, the Heavenly Calling of the Church (Vocalization), Chapters 1—3**
   A. The Church Is a Body, Chapter 1
      1. Introduction, Chapter 1:1–2
      2. God the Father Planned the Church, Chapter 1:3–6 ("A body hast thou prepared me")
      3. God the Son Paid the Price for the Church, Chapter 1:7–12 ("Redemption through His blood")
      4. God the Holy Spirit Protects the Church, Chapter 1:13–14 ("By one Spirit are we all baptized into one body")
      5. Prayer for Knowledge and Power, Chapter 1:15–23
   B. The Church Is a Temple, Chapter 2
      1. The Material for Construction, Chapter 2:1–10 (The "dead in trespasses" are made into a living temple)
      2. The Method of Construction, Chapter 2:11–18
      3. The Meaning of the Construction (quo animo), Chapter 2:19–22 ("Groweth unto an holy temple in the Lord")
   C. The Church Is a Mystery, Chapter 3
      1. The Explanation of the Mystery, Chapter 3:1–4 (Not revealed in the Old Testament)
      2. The Definition of the Mystery, Chapter 3:5–13 (Jews and Gentiles are partakers of the same Body—the Church)
      3. Prayer for Power and Knowledge, Chapter 3:14–21 ("Strengthened with might" and "to know the love of Christ")

II. Practical, the Earthly Conduct of the Church (Vocation), Chapters 4–6

  A. The Church Is a New Man, Chapter 4

    1. The Exhibition of the New Man, Chapter 4:1–6
    ("Endeavoring to keep the unity of the Spirit")

    2. The Inhibition of the New Man, Chapter 4:7–16
    ("No more children"—"grow up into Him"—"perfect man")

    3. The Prohibition of the New Man, Chapter 4:17–32
    ("Walk not as other Gentiles walk"—"be ye kind one to another")

  B. The Church Will Be a Bride, Chapter 5

    1. The Engagement of the Church, Chapter 5:1–17
    ("For I have espoused you to one husband, that I may present you as a chaste virgin to Christ")

    2. The Experience of the Church, Chapter 5:18–24
    ("Be filled with the Spirit")

    3. The Expectation of the Church, Chapter 5:25–33
    ("That he might present it to himself a glorious church")

  C. The Church Is a Soldier, Chapter 6

    1. The Soldier's Relationships, Chapter 6:1–9
    ("No man that warreth entangleth himself with the affairs of this life")

    2. The Soldier's Enemy, Chapter 6:10–12
    ("The wiles of the devil")

    3. The Soldier's Protection, Chapter 6:13–18
    ("The whole armour of God")

    4. The Soldier's Example—Paul, a Good Soldier of Jesus Christ, Chapter 6:19–22

    5. The Soldier's Benediction, Chapter 6:23–24

CHAPTER 1

THEME: The church is a body; Introduction; God the Father planned the church; God the Son paid the price for the church; God the Holy Spirit protects the church; prayer of Paul for knowledge and power for the Ephesians

Ephesians begins with the doctrinal section concerning the heavenly calling of the church, the vocalization.

INTRODUCTION

Paul, an apostle of Jesus Christ by the will of God, to the saints which are at Ephesus, and to the faithful in Christ Jesus:

Grace be to you, and peace, from God our Father, and from the Lord Jesus Christ [Eph. 1:1–2].

This is the briefest of all the introductions to Paul's epistles. It's brief because, very frankly, this epistle was sent to the church in Ephesus but was intended to be for all the churches. In some of the better manuscripts *en Epheso* is left out—it's not there. Ephesians was apparently the epistle that Paul referred to when he said in Colossians to read the epistle to the Laodiceans. In other words, this was a circular letter for the churches in that day. He's not writing here to the local church as much as he is to the church in general, that is, the invisible body of believers.

"Paul, an apostle of Jesus Christ" should be changed to Paul, an apostle of Christ Jesus. I hope you'll not think I'm splitting hairs here, but all the way through this epistle and in many other places it should be Christ Jesus. The word *Christ* is His title. That's who He is: ". . . Thou art the Christ, the Son of the living God" (Matt. 16:16). *Jesus* was His human name. Paul could say that "We know Him no longer after the flesh" (see 2 Cor. 5:16). Paul didn't know Him as the Jesus of the three-years' ministry but rather as the glorified Christ he met on the Damascus road. Paul always emphasized the name of *Christ* first—Christ Jesus.

Paul states that he is "an apostle." What is an apostle? It is the highest office the church has ever had. No one today is an apostle in the church for the simple reason that they cannot meet the requirements of an apostle. Here are the requirements: (1) The apostles received their commission directly from the living lips of Jesus. Paul made that claim for himself. He wrote, "Paul, an apostle, (not of men, neither by man, but by Jesus Christ, and God the Father, who raised him from the dead;)" (Gal. 1:1). This is the reason I believe Paul took the place of Judas. The disciples had selected Mathias, but I don't find anywhere that Jesus Christ made him an apostle. Apparently all the apostles received their commission directly from the Lord Jesus. (2) The apostle saw the Savior after His resurrection. Paul could meet that requirement. (3) The apostles exercised a special inspiration. They expounded and wrote Scripture (see John 14:26; 16:13; Gal. 1:11–12). Certainly Paul measures up to that more than any other apostle. (4) They exercised supreme authority (see John 20:22–23; 2 Cor. 10:8). (5) The badge of their authority was the power to work miracles (see Mark 6:13; Luke 9:1–2; Acts 2:43). I do not believe such power is invested in men today. That was the badge of an apostle. John wrote at the end of the first century, "If there come any unto you, and bring not this doctrine, receive him not into your house, neither bid him God speed" (2 John 10). The badge was no longer the ability to work miracles but having the right doctrine. (6) They were given a universal commission to found churches (see 2 Cor. 11:28). Paul expressly met these six requirements for apostleship.

"Paul, an apostle of Christ Jesus by the will of God." Paul rested his apostleship upon the will of God rather than any personal ambition or will of man or request of a church. He wrote to the Galatians: "But when it pleased *God*, who separated me from my mother's womb, and called me by his grace, to reveal his Son in me, that I might preach him among the heathen . . ." (Gal. 1:15–16, italics mine). Paul said to Timothy: "And I thank Christ Jesus our Lord, who hath enabled me, for that he counted me faithful, putting me into the ministry; who was before a blasphemer, and a persecutor, and injurious: but I obtained mercy, because I did it ignorantly in unbelief" (1 Tim. 1:12–13). Paul made constant reference to the will of God as the foundation of his apostleship. You can check 1 Corinthians 1:1; 2 Corinthians 1:1; Colossians 1:1; 2 Timothy 1:1. He says it in all these places.

"To the saints . . . at Ephesus." The word for saint is *hagios* which means "holy" or "separated." The primary intent of the word is "set aside for the sole use of God, that which belongs to God." The pots and pans in the tabernacle were called holy vessels. Why? Because they were especially holy and very fine and nice? No. I think they were all beat up and battered after that long wilderness journey. They were holy because they were for the use of God. A saint, my friend, is one who has trusted Christ and is set aside for the sole use of God. There are only two kinds of people today: the saints and the ain'ts. If you are a saint, then you are not an ain't. If you ain't an ain't, then you are a saint. Now there are some saints who are not being used of God. That is their fault. They are set aside for the use of God and for His service. Saints should act saintly, it's true. But they're not saints because of the way they act. They are saints because of their position in Christ. They belong to Him to be used of Him.

"At Ephesus." We have already referred to that. You can put in the name of your town here. For me it could be "at Pasadena."

"And to the faithful in Christ Jesus." These are the believers. The believers and the saints are the same, you see. A saint should be saintly and a believer should be faithful. A believer is one who has trusted Christ and a saint is the same one. The term *saint* is the God-ward aspect of the Christian. The term *believer* is the manward aspect of the Christian.

"In Christ Jesus." This is the most wonderful thing of all. This epistle is going to amplify that so much, that I will be dwelling on that in more detail later on. To me the most important word in the New Testament is the little preposition *in*. Theologians have come up with some "lulus" trying to tell us what it means to be saved. How do you define our salvation? There are words like redemption, atonement, justification, reconciliation, propitiation, and the vicarious, substitu-

tionary sacrifice of Christ. All of these words are good; they are wonderful, but each one of them merely gives one aspect of our salvation.
What does it really mean to be saved? It means to be *in Christ*. We are
irrevocably and organically joined to Christ by the baptism of the Holy
Spirit (see 1 Cor. 12:12–13). We are put into the body of believers. We
are told, ". . . he that is joined unto the Lord is one spirit" (1 Cor. 6:17).
We belong to Him, and there's nothing as wonderful as that. "There is
therefore now no condemnation to them which are in Christ Jesus . . ."
(Rom. 8:1). Can you improve on that? Being in Christ Jesus is the great
accomplishment of salvation. Dr. Lewis Sperry Chafer found that the
word *in* occurred one hundred and thirty times in the New Testament.
The Lord Jesus said, "Ye *in* me and I *in* you" (see John 15:4). How
wonderful! We are *in* Christ. I can't explain it; it's so profound. Analo-
gies may help us here:

> The bird is in the air; the air is in the bird.
> The fish is in the water; the water is in the fish.
> The iron is in the fire; the fire is in the iron.

The believer is in Christ and Christ is in the believer. We are joined
to Him. The head is in the body and the body is in the head. My body
can't move without the head directing it. The church, which is "the
body of Christ" is *in* Christ, the Head. All the truths of Ephesians
revolve around this fact.

Take time to look carefully at this epistle. I feel very keenly that
along with Romans, 1 and 2 Corinthians, and Galatians, Ephesians
should be given top priority among the epistles. I feel that these epistles have a throbbing, personal, living message for you and me today,
probably as no other portion of Scripture does. They are the great doctrinal epistles. When God said to Joshua, ". . . arise, go over this Jordan" (Josh. 1:2), I know He's not talking to me; but He is giving
instructions to Joshua. Yet, to me it has an application. The Epistle to
the Ephesians is the Book of Joshua of the New Testament, and it
speaks directly to me in a personal way.

"Grace be to you." *Grace* was the form of greeting of the Gentile
world in Paul's day. The Greek word was *charis*. Two men met on the

street and one would say to the other, "Charis." I walked down the streets of Athens with a Greek friend of mine who is a missionary. He spoke to several people as we went by, and I said to him, "It sounds to me like you greet them with the word *charis*." He laughed and said, "Well, it's similar to it." Apparently it's still a form of greeting today.

"And peace." The greeting in the religious world was "Peace." That is the word you hear in Jerusalem: "Shalom!"

Paul takes these two words which were the common greeting of the day and gives both of them a wonderful meaning and lifts them to the heights. The grace of God is the means by which He saves us. You must know the grace of God before you can experience the peace of God. Paul always puts them in that order—grace before peace. You must have grace before you can experience peace. "Therefore being justified by faith, we have peace with God through our Lord Jesus Christ" (Rom. 5:1).

You see the word *peace* everywhere today. Generally it refers to peace in some section of the world, or world peace. But the world can never know peace until it knows the grace of God. The interesting thing is, you don't see the word *grace* around very much. You see the word *love* and the word *peace*. They are very familiar words, and they are supposed to be taken from the Bible, but often they don't mean what they mean in the Word of God. *Peace* is peace with God because our sins are forgiven. Our sins can never be forgiven until we know something of the grace of God.

"From God our Father, and from the Lord Jesus Christ." The grace and peace are from God our Father. In fact, He becomes our Father when we experience the grace of God and are regenerated by the Spirit of God. Grace and peace also come from the Lord Jesus Christ. Why didn't Paul say they also came from the Holy Spirit? Doesn't Paul believe in the Trinity? Oh, yes, but the Holy Spirit was already in Ephesus indwelling believers. The Lord Jesus was seated at God's right hand in the heavens. We need to keep our geography straight when we study the Bible. A great many people get their theology warped because they don't have their geography right; and when we get that straightened out, it even helps our theology.

GOD THE FATHER PLANNED THE CHURCH

We come now to the second major division of the first chapter. It begins with a most marvelous verse.

Blessed be the God and Father of our Lord Jesus Christ, who hath blessed us with all spiritual blessings in heavenly *places* **in Christ [Eph. 1:3].**

We notice something that is very important here. He has blessed us. We praise Him with our lips because He first made us blessed. Our blessing is a declaration. His blessings are deeds. We pronounce Him blessed. He makes us blessed. The word blessed has in it the thought of happiness and joy. God is rejoicing today. He is happy because He has a way of saving you and He can bless you. It says He hath blessed us. I can't think of anything more wonderful than this. He is not speaking here of something that may be ours when we get to heaven but of something that is ours right now. Somebody says to me, "Have you had the second blessing?" Second blessing! My friend, I'm working way up in the hundreds—in fact, up in the thousands. I've not only had a second blessing; I've had a thousand blessings. He's blessed us, and He's done it in Christ.

"In heavenly places in Christ." You will notice that "places" is in italics in the text. It literally states, "in the heavenlies in Christ." Here we are, blessed with all spiritual blessings, and it is in the heavenlies. I don't know exactly where the heavenlies are, but I do know where the Lord Jesus is. He is at God's right hand, and we are told here that these blessings are in Christ. May I say to you that we need to be careful with this. It does not say here that these blessings are with Christ (there are those who read it like that). Right now you and I are seated in Christ. When somebody asks, "Are you going to heaven some day?" the answer generally given is, "Well, I hope so." Let me say this to you: if you're going to heaven, you're already there in Christ. He has blessed you in the heavenlies in Christ, and you are there regardless of what your position is down here. Your practice down here may not be good, but if you are a child of God, you are already in Christ.

Some people even misunderstand it in another way. I was teaching Ephesians at a conference once, and they called on a brother at the end of the service to lead the prayer. He started by saying, "Lord, we just thank you that this morning we've been sitting in the heavenly places in Christ." Well, he missed the point. We don't have to come to a Bible study (as important as that is) and have our hearts thrilled with these great spiritual truths to be sitting in the heavenlies. The fact of the matter is, you are in the heavenlies in Christ even when you are down in the dumps. Everyone who is in Christ is seated in the heavenlies in Him. That is the position which He has given to us.

"Blessed be the God and Father of our Lord Jesus Christ." We praise Him. Why? Because He has blessed us. He has blessed us with all spiritual blessings. The parallel here is Joshua in the Old Testament. We saw in the study of that book that Canaan was given to the children of Israel by God. Canaan is not a picture of heaven. Canaan is a picture of where we live today. It could never be heaven because there were enemies to be fought and battles to be won. Down here is where the battle is being fought. When we get to heaven, there will be no more battles. The interesting point here is that God gave them Canaan. All they had to do was lay hold of their possession. God told Joshua, "Every place that the sole of your foot shall tread upon, that have I given unto you, as I said unto Moses" (Josh. 1:3). Joshua could say, "Well, Lord, you've already given it to us. You let us walk in and take it."

My friend, God has blessed us with all spiritual blessings. We are in Christ. Have you ever stopped to think of what we have in Christ? Christ has been made unto us justification and sanctification. When I started out in church as a boy, I was working for my salvation. I didn't do very well with that. Then I learned that Christ is my justification. I tried to work to be good after I was saved, and I didn't do very well at that either. Then I learned that Christ has been made unto me sanctification. You see, I have everything in Christ; I have been blessed with all spiritual blessings. You can't improve on that, can you? When you come to Christ, you have everything in Him. Don't come and tell me today that I have to wait until later on, that I have to tarry for the Holy Spirit to give me something special—for example, a baptism. I have it all in Christ. When you tell me that I did not get everything in Christ, you are denying what Christ did for me. I got *everything* when I came to Him.

Now there are two ways to treat these blessings, which are actually your spiritual possessions: either to lay hold of them or not to lay hold of them. Two stories illustrate what I mean, and both of them are true. When I was in Chicago many years ago, I picked up the evening paper during the week and read a little article and clipped it out. It was way down at the bottom of the front page and wasn't apt to be noticed. It read: "The flophouses and saloons of Chicago's Skid Row were searched today for one Stanley William McKenna Walker, 50, an Oxford graduate and heir to half of an $8,000,000 English estate. The missing persons detail hoped that somewhere among the down-and-outers who line the curbs and sleep off wine binges in the cheap hotels they would find Walker, son of a wealthy British shipbuilder." I thought how tragic it was. Imagine being an heir to half of $8,000,000 and being a wino who's sleeping in two-bit hotels. I felt like sitting down and weeping for that poor fellow. Then I began thinking of the children of God today who are living in cheap hotels, living off the little "wine" of this world. I don't mean that literally, but that they engage in cheap entertainment down here. They are wealthy beyond the dreams of Croesus and are blessed with all spiritual blessings, but they live like paupers down here. There are a lot of folk in our churches who live like that today, and it's tragic. I was telling this story when I was a pastor in Los Angeles, and a lady who was visiting from Chicago came up afterward and asked, "Dr. McGee, do you know the end of that story?" I said, "No, I never heard." She said, "Well, they found him." "Oh," I replied, "that was wonderful." "No," she said, "they found him dead in a doorway on a cold night later on that fall." How tragic to die like that man died. Many Christians live and die like that, and yet they are blessed with all spiritual blessings in the heavenlies in Christ.

The second true story happened out West here, years ago. An heir to a British nobleman was living in poverty and barely eking out an existence. After the nobleman died, they began to look for his heir and when they found him, they told him about his inheritance. A great deal of publicity was made of it. Do you know what that fellow did? He immediately went down to the clothing store and ordered their best suit and then bought a first class ticket to return to England in style. Do you know why? He believed the inheritance was his, and he acted upon it. My friend, you can go either route. You can travel your Christian life in first class or in steerage. You can go second, third, or fourth class, and there are a lot of Christians doing that today. God wants you to know that you've been blessed with *all* spiritual blessings. He hasn't promised us physical blessings, but He has promised spiritual ones, and these are in the heavenlies in Christ. My friend, you're not going to have any spiritual blessing in this life that doesn't come to you through Jesus Christ. That's just how important He is. He not only has saved us, but He is also the One who blesses us. How we need to lay hold of Him today and to start living as a child of God should live!

We come now to a very important section. We are in that division of the outline which states that God the Father planned the church. You would not build a house today without a blueprint. What is God's blueprint? What did God do in planning for the church? We find in this section that He did three things: (1) He chose us in Christ; (2) He predestinated us to the place of sonship; and (3) He made us accepted in the Beloved.

Now I know that we have come to a passage of Scripture that is difficult. You'll have to gird up the loins of your mind because this is a very strong passage in the Word of God. We are going to talk about election and about predestination. These are two words that are frightening. Many people run for cover when they hear these words mentioned. But they are Bible words, and they have a meaning which is important for us to see.

> **According as he hath chosen us in him before the foundation of the world, that we should be holy and without blame before him in love [Eph. 1:4].**

This verse and the verses that follow are essentially the most difficult verses in Scripture to grasp. They are repulsive to the natural man, and the average believer finds them difficult to accept at face value. Although the statements are clear, the truth they contain is hard to receive. These verses are like a walnut—hard to crack but with a lot of goodies on the inside.

"According as" is a connective which modifies the preceding statement in verse three. The spiritual blessings which you and I are given are in accord with the divine will. All is done in perfect unison with God's purpose. This world and this universe *will* operate according to the plan and purpose of Almighty God. "According as" looks back to the three-in-one blessing of the last verse. There are actually and ought to be three *ins* in verse three. There is, first of all, "in all spiritual blessings," which are then wrapped "*in* the heavenlies," and finally put in the larger package of "*in* Christ." The whole thought is: Open your gift and see what God has done for you, and then move out in faith and lay hold of it and live today on the high plane to which God has brought you. He's made you a son and blessed you with all spiritual blessings. We need to live like that in the world today.

Now all this was according to His plan. God the Father planned the church, God the Son paid for the church, and God the Holy Spirit protects the church. The source of all our blessings is the God and Father of our Lord Jesus Christ. He carries our mind back to eternity past to make us realize that salvation is altogether of God and not at all of ourselves. You and I are not the originators or the promoters or the consummators of our salvation. God did it all. An old hymn puts it like this:

> 'Tis not that I did choose Thee
> For, Lord, that could not be.
> This heart would still refuse Thee
> But Thou hast chosen me.

A favorite hymn of today says:

> Jesus sought me when a stranger
> Wandering from the fold of God.
> He, to rescue me from danger,
> Interposed His precious blood.

"According as he hath chosen us in him before the foundation of the world." God planned our salvation way back yonder in eternity before you and I were even in this world at all. The Lord Jesus Christ is the One who came down in time, and He wrought out our salvation upon the cross when the fullness of time had come. God the Holy Spirit is the One who convicts us today. He brings us to the place of faith in Christ and to a saving knowledge of the grace of God that is revealed in the Lord Jesus Christ.

I heard this story many years ago. A black boy in Memphis, Tennessee, wanted to join a conservative, fundamental church, and the deacons were examining him. They asked him, "How did you get saved?" He answered, "I did my part, and God did His part." The deacons thought they had him, so they asked him what was his part and what was God's part. He said, "My part was the sinning. I ran from God as fast as these rebellious legs would take me and my sinful heart would lead me. I ran from Him. But you know, He done took out after me 'til He done run me down." My friend, there is nothing in a theology book that tells it as well as that. God is the One who did the saving. Our part was the sinning.

The late Dr. Harry A. Ironside told this story. A little boy was asked, "Have you found Jesus?" The little fellow answered, "Sir, I didn't know He was lost. But I was lost and He found me." My friend, you don't find Jesus. He finds you. He is the One who went out after the lost sheep, and He is the One who found that sheep.

God chose believers in Christ before the foundation of the world, way back in eternity past. That means that you and I didn't do the choosing. He did not choose us because we were good or because we would do some good, but He did choose us so that we *could* do some good. The entire choice is thrown back upon the sovereignty of the wisdom and goodness of God alone. It was Charles Spurgeon who once said, "God chose me before I came into the world, because if He'd waited until I got here, He never would have chosen me." It is God who has chosen us—we have not chosen Him. The Lord Jesus said to His own in the Upper Room, "Ye have not chosen me, but I have chosen you . . ." (John 15:16). Dr. G. Campbell Morgan commented, "That puts the responsibility on Him. If He did the choosing, then He's responsible." That makes it quite wonderful!

Israel furnishes us an example of this divine choosing. "Hear this word that the LORD hath spoken against you, O children of Israel, against the whole family which I brought up from the land of Egypt, saying, You only have I known of all the families of the earth: therefore I will punish you for all your iniquities" (Amos 3:1–2). God chose Israel in time; He chose the church in eternity. Since God made the choice in eternity, there has not arisen anything unforeseen to Him which has caused Him to revamp His program or change His mind. He knew the end from the beginning (see Acts 15:18).

God did all this for a purpose: "that we should be holy and without blame before him in love." God chose us in order to sanctify us. He saves us and He sanctifies us that we might be holy. That's the positive side of His purpose. It has to do with the inner life of the believer. A holy life is demanded by God's election. Now don't tell me that you can say, "Well, I'm one of the elected. I have been saved by grace, and now I can do as I please." Paul answered that kind of reasoning. "What shall we say then? Shall we continue in sin, that grace may abound? God forbid. How shall we, that are dead to sin, live any longer therein?" (Rom. 6:1–2). You can't use grace as a license to sin, my friend. If you go on living in sin, it is because you are a sinner who hasn't been saved. A sinner who has saved will show a change in his way of living.

Not only did God elect us in order that we should be holy but also that we should be "without blame." Now this is the negative side. The believer in Christ is seen before God as without blame. Again we see an example of this in Israel. God would not permit Balaam to curse Israel or to find fault with His people. "He hath not beheld iniquity in Jacob, neither hath he seen perverseness in Israel: the LORD his God is with him, and the shout of a king is among them" (Num. 23:21). Yes, but if you had gone down there into the camp of Israel, you would have found that God did find fault with them and He judged them— He was sanctifying and purifying that camp.

God has chosen you in order that He might make you holy and in order that He might make you without blame. It means that your life has been changed. If there is no evidence of change, then you are not one of the elect. God wants his children to live lives which are not marked or spotted with sin. He has made every provision to absolve them from all blame. "My little children, these things write I unto you, that ye sin not. And if any man sin, we have an advocate with the Father, Jesus Christ the righteous: and he is the propitiation for our sins: and not for ours only, but also for the sins of the whole world" (1 John 2:1–2).

By the way, that answers once and for all the question of a limited atonement, that is, that Christ died only for the elect. This verse in 1 John makes it clear that He died for the world. I don't care who you are, there is a legitimate offer that has been sent out to you today from God, and that offer is that Jesus Christ has died for you. You can't hide and say, "I am not one of the elect." You are of the elect if you hear His voice. You also have free will not to hear His voice. It is a glorious and wonderful thing that the God of heaven would elect some of us down here and save us. I don't propose to understand all that—I just believe it.

The Lord gave us a picture of a great big, wide highway and off that highway is a little, narrow entrance. Over the entrance it says, ". . . I am the way, the truth, and the life: no man cometh unto the Father, but by me" (John 14:6), and "I am the door . . ." (John 10:9). Now the interesting thing is that the broad highway on which most of the people are traveling leads down and gets narrower and narrower until finally it leads to destruction. You can keep on that broad highway if you wish, but you can also turn off if you want to. You can turn off at the invitation, ". . . him that cometh to me I will in no wise cast out" (John 6:37). You can enter in at that narrow way, and the interesting thing is that the entrance is narrow, but then the road widens out. ". . . I am come that they might have life, and that they might have it more abundantly" (John 10:10). You talk about the broad way! The broad way comes after you get through the narrow gate. But, you see, you must make the choice. Whosoever will may come—that includes you. It is a legitimate invitation.

D. L. Moody put it in his quaint way. He said, "The whosoeverwills are the elect and the whosoeverwon'ts are the nonelect." It is up to you. The Lord has extended the invitation. Whosoever will may come. Don't try to say that you are left out. God so loved the *world*. *Whosoever* believeth in Him shall not perish. That "whosoever" means J. Vernon McGee. It means you—you can put your name right in there. Just because there are the elect, it does not mean we know who they are. You have no right to say that you are of the nonelect. If you will open your heart, you can come. That is all you have to do. I don't believe in the idea today that you can have "mental reservations." The problem is that you have sin in your life, and the Bible condemns it. If you come to Christ, it means you'll have to turn from that sin, and some folk just don't want to turn from their sin.

"Chosen us in him." Again and again the Word of God emphasizes God's sovereign choice. Paul states, "But we are bound to give thanks always to God for you, brethren beloved of the Lord, because God hath from the beginning chosen you to salvation through sanctification of the Spirit and belief of the truth: whereunto he called you by our gospel, to the obtaining of the glory of our Lord Jesus Christ" (2 Thess. 2:13–14). Peter writes in 1 Peter 1:2, "Elect according to the foreknowledge of God the Father, through sanctification of the Spirit, unto obedience and sprinkling of the blood of Jesus Christ. . . ." The interesting thing is that election and sanctification seem to go together and they are both in the Lord Jesus Christ. If God has saved you, He hasn't saved you because you are good but because you are not good. Paul puts it in such a marvelous way: "What shall we say then? Is there unrighteousness with God? God forbid. For he saith to Moses, I will have mercy on whom I will have mercy, and I will have compassion on whom I will have compassion. So then it is not of him that willeth, nor of him that runneth, but of God that sheweth mercy" (Rom. 9:14–16). Moses had gone to God in prayer, and God had answered, "Moses, I am going to hear and answer your prayer, but it is not because you are Moses and the deliverer. It is because I will show mercy on whom I will and I'll show compassion on whom I will. It is not to him that wills or to him that works but it is I who shows compassion." Now, do you want to experience the compassion of God? Then you will have to turn to Him.

I think the best illustration of this is over in Acts 27. You remember that Paul was in a ship and there was a terrific storm so that the ship was listing and about ready to go down. They had already cast some of the cargo overboard to lighten the ship. Then Paul went to the captain and said, "And now I exhort you to be of good cheer: for there shall be no loss of any man's life among you, but of the ship. For there stood by me this night the angel of God, whose I am, and whom I serve, saying, Fear not, Paul; thou must be brought before Caesar: and, lo, God hath given thee all them that sail with thee" (Acts 27:22–24). Now that was God's foreknowledge. That is election. God had elected that nobody on that ship would be lost. Just a little later, Paul found a group of the sailors about to let down a lifeboat into the sea. They intended to go overboard, hoping to get to land in that way. Then Paul said to the captain, ". . . Except these abide in the ship, ye cannot be saved" (Acts 27:31). The captain could have said, "Wait a minute. You already told me that none would perish," and he would have been right. That is what Paul had said. That was God's side of it—none would perish. But the condition was, "Except these abide in the ship, ye cannot be saved." That was man's side of it—they had to stay in the ship.

Now God knows who the elect are. I don't. Someone came to Spurgeon one time and said, "Mr Spurgeon, if I believed as you do, I would not preach like you do. You say you believe that there are the elect, and yet you preach as if everybody can be saved." Spurgeon's answer was, "They can all be saved. If God had put a yellow streak up and down the backs of the elect, I'd go up and down the streets lifting up shirt tails to find out who had the yellow streak up and down his back. Then I'd give that person the gospel. But God didn't do that. He told me to preach the gospel to every creature and that whosoever will may come." That is our marching order, and as far as I am concerned, until God gives me the roll call of the elect, I am going to preach the "whosoever will" gospel. That is the gospel we are to preach today.

Someone else has put it like this. On the door to heaven, from our side, it says, "Whosoever will may enter. I am the door: by Me if any man. . . ." *Any man*—that means *you*. You can come in and find pasture and find life. When you get on the other side of the door someday in heaven, you're going to look back, and on that door you will find written, "Chosen in Him before the foundation of the world." I haven't seen that side of the door yet; therefore, I give God (since He is God) the right to plan *His* church.

A friend of mine down in Florida once showed me the blueprint of a home he was going to build. He had planned it and had it all marked out in the blueprint. They had only laid the foundation, but he and his wife showed me where everything was going to be. Later on when we were in that home to visit them, it was just like they planned it. They didn't have supernatural knowledge, but as far as I know, no one has questioned whether they had the right to do that or not. They did have the right, and they did it according to their plan. God has planned the church. After all, this is His universe, and the church is His church. What is His plan? "According as he hath chosen us in him before the foundation of the world, that we should be holy and without blame before him in love."

Now the words *in love* are not connected with verse four, but actually with verse five. "In love,"

Having predestinated us unto the adoption of children by Jesus Christ to himself, according to the good pleasure of his will [Eph. 1:5].

Somebody says, "Oooh, there's that word *predestination,* and that's another frightful term!" Friend, that's one of the most *wonderful* words we have in Scripture, and this a glorious section. It is something we don't hear too much about today. If I were not going through the Bible, I would have probably avoided this and would have chosen something else. I would have talked about the comfort there is for the saints, which is the big theme of even most fundamental preachers today. We're all talking about comfort, but what we have here is strong medicine. Some folk won't be able to take the medicine; but if you take it, it'll do you good. We need something pretty strong in this flabby age in which we live. We need to *know* that we've been chosen in Him in order to stand for God today. It will make a world of difference in your life.

We are treading on the mountaintops in Ephesians. We're in eternity past when God planned the church. I wasn't back there to give Him any suggestions or tell Him how I wanted it done, but He's telling me how He did it. In essence, God says to you and me, "You either take it or leave it. This is the way I did it. Maybe you don't like it, but this is the way I did it, and I'm the One who is running this universe, you see." God hasn't turned it over to any political party yet. Thank God for that! He hasn't turned it over to any individual either. We can thank Him for that. He certainly hasn't turned it over to me, and I tell you, all of us can shout a hearty "Amen" to that and thank Him He didn't do it that way. God has done three things for us, however, in planning the church. First of all, we've seen that He chose us—and that's a pretty hard pill for us to swallow. Secondly, the Father predestinated us to the place of sonship. Thirdly, the Father made us accepted in the Beloved.

I cannot repeat often enough that election is God's choosing us in Christ. I emphasize again that men are not lost because they have not been elected. They are lost because they are sinners and that is the way they want it and that is the way they have chosen. The free will of man is never violated because of the election of God. The lost man makes his own choice. Augustine expressed it like this: "If there be not free will grace in God, how can He save the world? And if there be not free will in man, how can the world by God be judged?" Here again is Paul's strong statement, "What shall we say then? Is there unrighteousness with God? God forbid" (Rom. 9:14). Now if you think that there is some unrighteousness with God, you had better change your mind.

I get the impression in some of the evangelistic campaigns today that people are asked to come forward and even that coming forward is doing something. May I say to you that God says He is not saving any of us because we came forward, or because we are nice little boys or nice little girls, or because we have joined a church, or even because we have an inclination to turn to Him. God says that it is because He extends mercy. He had to say that even to Moses. Moses could have gone to the Lord and said, "Look, I'm Moses. I'm leading the children of Israel out of Egypt. I'm really up there at the top. You'd have a problem getting along without me. Therefore, I want You to hear my prayer." If you read his prayers, Moses never prayed like that. It was God who said, "I will have mercy on whom I will have mercy and compassion on whom I will have compassion." He told Moses that He was going to hear and answer his prayer, but not because he was Moses, but because ". . . it is not of him that willeth, nor of him that runneth, but of God that sheweth mercy" (Rom. 9:16).

My friend, I'm going to be in heaven someday, and I'm not going to be there because Vernon McGee is a nice little boy. He's not. You don't know me like I know myself. If you knew me, you would tune me out right now. But wait a minute—don't tune me out, because if I knew you like you know yourself, I wouldn't even speak to you. So let's stay together, shall we? We are both in the same boat—we are all lost sinners. I will not be in heaven because I am a preacher or because I joined a church. It will not be because I was baptized. I have been sprinkled *and* immersed. My wife belonged to a Southern Baptist church and she has always prided herself on being immersed. I tease her and say it sure will be funny if we get to heaven and find out the Lord really meant sprinkled after all. I tell her that that would leave her out, but I'm safe because I've been baptized both ways. You see, that is ridiculous—none of those things will put a person into heaven. The only reason I am going to be in heaven is because of the mercy of God. I am a lost sinner. Until you and I are willing to come to God as a nobody and then let Him make us a somebody, you and I will never be saved.

> Your best resolutions must totally be waived,
> Your highest ambitions be crossed.
> You need never think that you will ever be saved,
> Until first you have learned that you're lost.

It is to the lost sinner that God is prepared to extend His mercy.

Don't tell me you have "intellectual problems"—hurdles to get over. The problem with you and the problem with me was not that we had trouble with Jonah, or with Noah and the ark. Our problem today is that the Bible condemns the sin in our lives. God will save you when your heart is willing to turn to Him. He's planned it like this in order that He might bring you and me into heaven someday; and when we get there, we are going to find out that He's the One who did it.

Now in verse five we come to the next thing God did for us. "In love having predestinated us." Some are going to say that they never knew you could get predestination and love together even in the same county, let alone in the same verse. But here they are. God's love is involved in this word which has been frightful to a great many people. The word *predestination* comes from the Greek *proorisos*, and it literally means "to define, to mark out, to set apart." It means "to horizon." If you go outside and look around (especially if you're in flat country), you only can see to the horizon. You're "horizoned"; you're put in that area. When it refers to God, predestination has to do with God's purpose with those He chooses.

Predestination is never used in reference to unsaved people. God has never predestinated anybody to be lost. If you are lost, it is because you have rejected God's remedy. It is like a dying man to whom the doctor offers curing medicine. "If you take this, it'll heal you." The man looks at the doctor in amazement and says, "I don't believe you." Now the man dies and the doctor's report says he died of a certain disease, and that's accurate. But may I say to you, there was a remedy, and he actually died because he didn't take the remedy. God has provided a remedy. Let me repeat, God has never predestined anybody to be lost. That's where your free will comes in, and you have to determine for yourself what your choice will be.

Predestination refers only to those who are saved. What it actually means is that when God starts out with one hundred sheep, He is going to come through with one hundred sheep. "And we know that all things work together for good to them that love God, to them who are the called according to his purpose. For whom he did foreknow, he also did predestinate to be conformed to the image of his Son, that he might be the firstborn among many brethren" (Rom. 8:28–29). Dr. R. A. Torrey used to say that this is a wonderful pillow for a tired heart. Those who are called according to His purpose are predestinated to be conformed to the image of His Son. We're talking now about saved people. Romans goes on to explain how this is done. "Moreover whom he did predestinate, them he also called: and whom he called, them he also justified: and whom he justified, them he also glorified" (Rom. 8:30). When God starts out with one hundred sheep, He will come through with one hundred sheep. You must admit that that is a good percentage.

Years ago I was told by a sheep rancher in San Angelo, Texas, that he would appreciate coming out with 65 percent. He said, "We can make money if we get to market 65 percent of the sheep that we start out with." That makes you feel that it wouldn't hurt too much if one little sheep got lost.

The Lord Jesus told a parable about a man who had one hundred sheep, and one little sheep got lost. You know, most of us get lost even after we have been saved. That doesn't mean we lose our salvation, but we surely get out of fellowship with Him. Some people can get lost so far that they actually fear they have lost their salvation. But the little lost sheep is still a sheep even though he is way out yonder and lost. "All we like sheep have gone astray . . ." (Isa. 53:6). That's our propensity; that's our tendency; that's the direction we go. We don't go toward God, but we go away from Him. So what does the Shepherd do? He goes out to look for that one lost sheep! I'm confident that the man who raised sheep in Texas wouldn't get up and go out into a cold, blustery, stormy night to get one little sheep. I think he would say, "Let him go." Thank God, we have a Shepherd who never says that! He says, "I started out with one hundred sheep and I'm going to come through with that one hundred sheep." Now, suppose the day comes when He is counting His sheep up in heaven, way out there somewhere in the future. He starts out, "One, two, three, four, five . . . ninety-six, ninety-seven, ninety-eight, ninety-nine, ninety-nine, ninety-nine—what in the world happened to Vernon McGee? Well, We've just lost one, so We'll let it go at that. A lot of folk didn't think Vernon McGee was going to make it anyway." Thank God, He will not do it that way. If I am not there when He counts in His sheep, He is going to go out and look for me, and He is going to bring me in. That is what predestination means. I *love* that word. It is God's guarantee.

"My sheep hear my voice, and I know them, and they follow me: and I give unto them eternal life; and they shall never perish, neither shall any man pluck them out of my hand" (John 10:27-28). Always remember that if sheep are saved, it is not because they are smart little sheep. They are stupid little fellows. If they are safe, it is because they have a wonderful Shepherd. That is the glorious truth.

We are predestinated "unto the adoption of the children by Jesus Christ to himself." Adoption means that we are brought into the place of full-grown sons. We have dealt with that in the Epistle to the Galatians. It implies two very important things. Adoption into sonship means regeneration. We have been regenerated by the Spirit of God. The child of God has been born again ". . . not of corruptible seed, but of incorruptible, by the word of God, which liveth and abideth for ever" (1 Pet. 1:23). He is born again into a new relationship. That is what the Lord Jesus meant when He told Nicodemus that he must be born again. Adoption also means a place of position and privilege. When we are saved, we are born into the family of God as a babe in Christ; but, in addition, we are given the position of an adult son. We are in a position where we can understand the Word of the Father because He has given us the Holy Spirit as our Teacher.

When my little grandson was almost two years old, he talked constantly, but I could understand only a few words that he said. Yet I could pretty well tell what he wanted and needed. He was just a little, bitty fellow and he couldn't understand why I didn't know what he was saying. He didn't always understand me either, by the way. The wonderful thing is that I have a Heavenly Father today—and I've been a babe a long time—and He's told me that He's put me in a position where I can understand Him. How wonderful it's going to be as my grandson grows up and we can really understand one another. God, however, communicates to us now. Paul tells us how: "Now we have received, not the spirit of the world, but the spirit which is of God; that we might know the things that are freely given to us of God" (1 Cor. 2:12). All of this is done in Christ Jesus. "For there is one God, and one mediator between God and men, the man Christ Jesus" (1 Tim. 2:5).

To the praise of the glory of his grace, wherein he hath made us accepted in the beloved [Eph. 1:6].

Since all is for the glory of God, Paul sings this glorious doxology, this wonderful psalm of praise. All is done on the basis of His grace and the end is the glory of God. The inception is grace; the conception is adoption; the reception is for His glory.

"Wherein he hath made us accepted in the beloved." Who is the Beloved? It is the Lord Jesus Christ. It is the Lord Jesus who said, "Father, I will that they also, whom thou hast given me, be with me where I am; that they may behold my glory, which thou hast given me: for thou lovedst me before the foundation of the world" (John 17:24). God sees the believer in Christ and He accepts the believer just as He receives His own Son. That is wonderful. That is the only basis on which I will be in heaven. I cannot stand there on the merit of Vernon McGee. I am accepted only in the Beloved. God loves me just as He loves Christ, because I am in Christ. Jesus said, "I in them, and thou in me, that they may be made perfect in one; and that the world may know that thou hast sent me, and hast loved them, as thou hast loved me" (John 17:23).

There has been, therefore, a threefold work performed by God the Father. He chose us in Christ. He predestinated us to the place of sonship. He has made us accepted in the Beloved. It is all to the praise of the glory of His grace. He is the One who gets the praise. He is the One who did it all.

All of this is for your good and my good. I just like to revel in this, I like to rejoice in this, and I talk about this because it is worth talking about. It is so much more valuable than a lot of the chitchat that I hear today that goes under the name of religion. How we need to see the grace of God as it is revealed in Christ!

GOD THE SON PAID THE PRICE FOR THE CHURCH

In whom we have redemption through his blood, the forgiveness of sins according to the riches of his grace [Eph. 1:7].

Back in eternity past God chose us, predestinated us, and made us accepted in the Beloved. Now we move out of eternity into time, where the plans of God the Father are placed into the hands of Christ, who moves into space and time to construct the church.

It is an historical fact that Jesus was born into this world over nineteen hundred years ago. God intruded into humanity and after being on this earth for thirty-three years, He died upon a cross, was buried, rose again bodily, and ascended into heaven. Those are the historical facts that the Word of God gives us. While He was here, He redeemed us, and that redemption is through His blood. This is something which is not popular today. Most people want a beautiful religion, one that appeals to their esthetic nature. The cross of Christ does not appeal to the esthetic part of man; it doesn't appeal to the pride of man. Unfortunately, the liberal churches and even a few so-called Bible churches make an appeal to the old nature of man and, therefore, there is no emphasis on the blood of Christ—it is considered repulsive.

Years ago a lady came up to the late Dr. G. Campbell Morgan. She was one of these dowagers who had a lorgnette (a lorgnette is a sneer on the end of a stick). She looked at him through her lorgnette and said, "Dr. Morgan, I don't like to hear about the blood. It is repulsive to me and offends my esthetic nature." Dr. Morgan replied, "I agree with you that it is repulsive, but the only thing repulsive about it is your sin and mine." Sin is the thing that is repulsive about the blood redemption, my friend.

A new pastor came to a great church in Washington, D.C., and a couple came to him and said, "We trust that you will not put too much emphasis on the blood. The former pastor we had talked a great deal about the blood, and we hope that you will not emphasize it too much." He answered, "You can be assured that I won't emphasize it too much." They looked pleased and thanked him for it. He said, "Wait a minute. It is not possible to emphasize it too much." And he continued to stress the blood. It is repulsive to man, but it is through His blood that we have redemption.

After God the Father had drawn the blueprint, the Son came to this earth to form the church with nail-pierced hands. The entire context of the Old Testament sets forth the expiation of sins by the blood of an animal sacrifice. Yet this could not take away sins—only Christ could execute that. The writer to the Hebrews says it this way: "In burnt offerings and sacrifices for sin thou hast had no pleasure. Then said I, Lo, I come (in the volume of the book it is written of me,) to do thy will, O God. Above when he said, Sacrifice and offering and burnt offerings and offering for sin thou wouldest not, neither hadst pleasure therein; which are offered by the law; then said he, Lo, I come to do thy will, O God. He taketh away the first, that he may establish the second. By the which will we are sanctified through the offering of the body of Jesus Christ once for all. And every priest standeth daily ministering and offering oftentimes the same sacrifices, which can never take away sins: but this man, after he had offered one sacrifice for sins for ever, sat down on the right hand of God; from henceforth expecting till his enemies be made his footstool" (Heb. 10:6–13).

"In whom we have redemption." "In whom" refers to the Beloved, who is Christ. We are accepted in the Beloved, in Christ. Redemption is the primary work of Christ. The literal here is "In whom we have the redemption." The word the gives it prominence, and the fact that it is named first gives it top priority. This is the reason Christ came to earth. "Even as the Son of man came not to be ministered unto, but to minister, and to give his life a ransom for many" (Matt. 20:28). He came to pay a price for your redemption and mine. We were slaves in sin, and He came to deliver us and give us liberty by paying a price for us.

There are three Greek words in the New Testament which are translated by the one English word redemption. The Greek word agorazo means "to buy at the marketplace." Here is the picture of a housewife out in the morning shopping for the day. She sees some vegetables and a roast and puts down cash on the barrelhead. She pays the price and now they belong to her, of course. The only thought in this word agorazo, then, is to buy and take out. This is the word Paul used in 1 Corinthians 6:20: "For ye are bought with a price: therefore glorify God in your body, and in your spirit, which are God's."

The Greek word exagorazo means "to buy out of the market," and it has the thought of buying something for one's own use. You see, somebody could go into the marketplace and buy that roast and those vegetables and go down to the next town, where they are short of those items, and put them up for sale at a profit. *Exagorazo* means, however, to take goods out of the market place and never to sell them again, but rather to keep them for one's own use. This is the word which is used in Galatians 3:13: "Christ hath redeemed us from the curse of the law, being made a curse for us: for it is written, Cursed is every one that hangeth on a tree." This means that Christ redeemed us so that we would not be exposed for sale again. He has paid the price, and He has taken us off the market. We belong to Him.

The third Greek word for redemption is *apolutrosis* which is the word used here in verse seven. It means "to liberate by the paying of a ransom in order to set a person free." It carries this same meaning in Luke 21:28: "And when these things begin to come to pass, then look up, and lift up your heads; for your redemption draweth nigh." *Redemption* is a marvelous word. It means not only to go into the marketplace and put cash on the barrelhead; it means not only to take it out of the market for your own private use, never to sell it to anyone else; but it also means to set free or to liberate after paying the price. The last applies to buying a slave out of slavery in order to set him free, and this is the word for redemption we have here in this verse. Man has been sold under sin and is in the bondage of sin. All one needs to do is look around to see that this is true. Man is a rotten, corrupt sinner and he cannot do anything else but sin—he is a slave to sin. Christ came to pay the price of man's freedom. That is what the Lord Jesus meant when He said, "If the Son therefore shall make you free, ye shall be free indeed" (John 8:36).

This redemption is "through his blood"—that was the price which He paid. "Forasmuch as ye know that ye were not redeemed with corruptible things, as silver and gold, from your vain conversation received by tradition from your fathers; but with the precious blood of Christ, as of a lamb without blemish and without spot" (1 Pet. 1:18–19). The blood of Christ is more valuable than silver and gold. For one thing, there is not much of it. A limited supply increases the value of a substance, but that really is not the reason for its value. One drop of the blood of the holy Son of God can save every sinner on topside of this earth, if that sinner will put his trust in the Savior. We have redemption through His blood, and the reason He saves us in that way is because ". . . without shedding of blood is no remission" (Heb. 9:22). This is an Old Testament principle which is applicable to the entire human race from Adam down to the last man. We have been redeemed now, not with the blood of bulls and goats—that can't redeem you—but with the precious blood of Christ.

"The forgiveness of sins." Forgiveness is not the act of an indulgent deity who is moved by sentiment to the exclusion of justice, righteousness, and holiness. Forgiveness depends on the shedding of blood: it demands and depends on the payment of the penalty for sin. Christ's death and the shedding of His blood is the foundation for forgiveness and, without that, there could be no forgiveness.

I think here we need to learn the distinction between human forgiveness and divine forgiveness—they are not the same. Human forgiveness is always based on the fact that a penalty is deserved and that the penalty is not imposed. It simply means that one wipes out the account. God is holy and righteous. Therefore divine forgiveness is always based on the fact that there has been the execution of the penalty and the price has been paid. Human forgiveness comes before the penalty is executed. Divine forgiveness depends upon the penalty being executed. It is really too bad that this is something which has bogged down our entire legal system today. That is why we are living in a lawless nation where it is not even safe to be on the streets of our cities at night. There has been a confusion between human forgiveness and the righteousness of the law. We are in trouble because of the leniency on the part of certain judges throughout our land. They sit on the bench and think they are being bighearted by letting the criminals go free. My friend, the righteousness of the law demands that a penalty must be paid. I once heard a judge say, "If God can forgive, then I can forgive." But God paid the penalty and then He forgave. Is the judge on the bench willing to go and pay the penalty? I don't think you have any right to take men out of death row unless you are willing to take their place, because a penalty must be executed.

A righteous God forgives on the basis that a penalty has been executed. When was it executed? When Jesus Christ shed His blood over nineteen hundred years ago. Sure, that's not esthetic. It doesn't appeal to the refined nature of civilized man today. Of course it doesn't—man thinks his sin doesn't really seem so bad. He tries to be sophisticated; he thinks he is suave and very clever. Friend, we are lost, hell-doomed sinners, and God cannot forgive us until the penalty has been executed. The good news is that the penalty has been executed. That is the reason that in the Word of God you will find forgiveness back to back with the blood of Jesus Christ. Forgiveness depends on the blood of Christ. That is how valuable His blood is. I have said it before, and I will say it again: you come to God as a nobody and let Him make you a somebody. He can forgive you your sins because He paid the penalty for your sins. This is the only way that you and I can have forgiveness for our sins.

The Lord Jesus said to His disciples, ". . . Thus it is written, and thus it behoved Christ to suffer, and to rise from the dead the third day: and that repentance and remission of sins should be preached in his name among all nations, beginning at Jerusalem" (Luke 24:46–47). Paul says the same thing in Colossians 1:14: "In whom we have redemption through his blood, even the forgiveness of sins." When Jesus met Paul on the Damascus road, He told him to go to the Gentiles, "to open their eyes, and to turn them from darkness to light, and from the power of Satan unto God, that they may receive forgiveness of sins, and inheritance among them which are sanctified by faith that is in me" (Acts 26:18). The shedding of the blood of Christ and His death on the cross is the foundation for forgiveness—*sine qua non* or without this there is nothing. God cannot forgive until the penalty has been paid.

The word for *sins* is *paraptoma* which means "an offense or a falling aside." Paul describes the first sin of man as an offense in Romans 5:15. He uses the same word in Romans 4:25, "Who was delivered for our offences and was raised again for our justification." "Sins" includes the entire list of sins which is chargeable to man. Augustine stated it succinctly: "Christ bought the church foul that He might make it fair." He bought it with His own blood and paid the penalty for our sin.

"According to the riches of his grace." That is an interesting expression. It doesn't say *out of* riches of His grace but *according to* the riches of His grace. Let me illustrate the difference. I read many years ago that when the late John D. Rockefeller played golf in Florida he always gave the caddy a dime. I always felt that that must have almost broke the man to pay out such an handsome sum. You see, he didn't give according to his riches—he gave out of his riches. I think he could have done a little better than that, and if he had paid according to his riches, the caddy would have been rich. God has redeemed us according to the riches of His grace. God is rich in grace, and He is willing to give according to His riches of grace. He has had to bestow so much on me, but He has enough left for you who are reading this way up in Alaska. It may be cold up there, but God's grace is rich up there. Some of you across the Pacific may read this, and He has grace for you. God can save you, and He can keep you, and it is due to His grace.

We are dealing with the work of God the Son on behalf of the church. That work is threefold: (1) Christ redeemed us through His blood; (2) He has revealed the mystery of His will; and (3) He rewards us with an inheritance.

We looked at the Greek words for redemption and saw that it involved the paying of a price which was the blood of Christ: we can have forgiveness because He paid the price. We know that God went into the marketplace where we were sold on the slave block of sin and He bought us, all of us. He is going to use us for Himself—He establishes a personal relationship. We saw also that He bought us in order to set us free. Now somebody will ask, "Doesn't that upset the hymn that says, 'I gave, I gave My life for thee. What hast thou done for Me?'?" My friend, it surely does. The very word for *redemption* in verse seven, *apolutrosis*, means that God never asks you what you have done for Him. That is the glorious thing about grace: when God saves you by grace, it doesn't put you in debt to Him. He bought you in order to set you free.

Someone else will ask, "But aren't we supposed to serve Him?" Certainly. But it is on another basis, a new relationship—the relationship now is love. The Lord Jesus said, "If ye love me, keep my commandments" (John 14:15). He didn't say, "Because I'm dying for you,

you are to keep My commandments." He said, "If you love Me." Today, if you love Him, He wants your service. If you don't love Him, then forget about this business of service. One hears so much today about commitment to Christ. Friend, you and I have very little to commit to Him. We are to respond in love to Him, and that is a different basis altogether. We love Him because He first loved us.

I heard this story many years ago, and it's the kind of story that you are not supposed to tell today, but I still tell it. I guess I'm still a square. It illustrates a great truth. In the South—and I hate to say, in the days of slavery—there was a beautiful girl who was put on the slave block to be sold. There was a very cruel slave owner, a brutal fellow, who began to bid for her. Every time he would bid, the girl would cringe and a look of fear would come over her face. A plantation owner who was kind to his slaves was there, and he began to bid for the girl. He outbid the other fellow and purchased her. He put down the price and started to walk away. The girl followed him, but he turned to her and said, "You misunderstand. I didn't buy you because I needed a slave. I bought you to set you free." She simply stood there, stunned for just a moment. Then she suddenly fell to her knees. "Why," she said, "I will serve you forever!" Now that illustrates the basis on which the Lord Jesus wants us to serve Him. He loved you. He paid a price for you. He gave Himself and shed His blood so that you could have forgiveness of sins. This is all yours if you are willing to come to Him and accept Him as your Savior.

Now what if someone says, "But I don't love Him." Then He is not asking you to serve Him. But if you do love Him, then He wants you to serve Him. That is what it is all about. Never forget, your redemption and your forgiveness are "according to the riches of his grace."

Now we are ready for the second work of God the Son on behalf of the church: Christ revealed the mystery of His will.

> **Wherein he hath abounded toward us in all wisdom and prudence;**
>
> **Having made known unto us the mystery of his will, according to his good pleasure which he hath purposed in himself:**

> That in the dispensation of the fulness of times he might
> gather together in one all things in Christ, both which
> are in heaven, and which are on earth; even in him
> [Eph. 1:8–10].

What is a mystery in Scripture? It is not a whodunit or a mystery story, and it is not something you wonder about, like, *Was it the butler who committed the crime?* It is not something Agatha Christie wrote or a Sherlock Holmes story, by any means. A mystery in Scripture means that God is revealing something that, up to that time, He had not revealed. There are two elements which always enter into a New Testament mystery: (1) It cannot be discovered by human agencies, for it is always a revelation from God; and (2) it is revealed at the proper time and not concealed, and enough is revealed to establish the fact without all the details being disclosed.

The *Scofield Reference Bible* (p. 1014) lists eleven mysteries in the New Testament:

> The greater mysteries are: (1) the mysteries of the kingdom of heaven (Mat. 13:3–50); (2) the mystery of Israel's blindness during this age (Rom. 11:25, with context); (3) the mystery of the translation of living saints at the end of this age (1 Cor. 15:51–52; 1 The. 4:13–17); (4) the mystery of the N.T. Church as one body composed of Jews and Gentiles (Eph. 3:1–12; Rom. 16:25; Eph. 6:19; Col. 4:3); (5) the mystery of the Church as the bride of Christ (Eph. 5:23–32); (6) the mystery of the in-living Christ (Gal. 2:20; Col. 1:26–27); (7) the "mystery of God even Christ," i.e., Christ as the incarnate fullness of the Godhead embodied, in whom all the divine wisdom for man subsists (1 Cor. 2:7; Col. 2:2,9); (8) the mystery of the processes by which godlikeness is restored to man (1 Tim. 3:16); (9) the mystery of iniquity (2 The. 2:7; cp. Mt. 13:33); (10) the mystery of the seven stars (Rev. 1:20); and (11) the mystery of Babylon (Rev. 17:5,7).

Yet, even with all these, did you know that God hasn't told us everything? There are a lot of things God hasn't told us. There are many questions that I would like to ask God myself. A great many people send us questions, and we attempt to answer them. I have questions, too, but I don't know who to ask because nobody down here knows the answers. Someday He will reveal them to us.

A mystery then is something God hasn't previously revealed but now reveals to us. Now in these verses is a wonderful mystery that was not revealed in the Old Testament. First let me restate verses eight and nine to amplify their meaning somewhat: "Which He caused (made) to abound toward us: having made known [aorist tense] unto us in all wisdom and prudence the mystery of His will, according to His good pleasure which He purposed in Him (Christ)." Notice that "in all wisdom and prudence" properly belongs with verse nine. What is the mystery of His will? First of all, it is something which is revealed according to wisdom and prudence. It is not some simple little "a-b-c" something. I very frankly rejoice that there are so many agencies and individuals who try to get out what they call the "simple gospel." I thank the Lord that people write and tell us that we are making the gospel simple and they can understand it. I appreciate that because that is what we must do. Dr. H. A. Ironside used to say, "Put the cookies on the bottom shelf where the kiddies can get to them." There is a "simple gospel" but, may I say to you, there are the depths and the wisdom of God that you and I can't easily probe— sometimes not at all. We need to use all the mental acumen that we have in order to try to understand something of the great purposes of God, the plan of God. God wants us to know these things because now this mystery has been revealed.

"That in the dispensation of the fulness of times he might gather together in one all things in Christ." *Dispensation* is another word like *mystery*. It is often misunderstood, and a great many people today think it is a dirty word. It is a great word! Some Bible teachers won't even use the word because it is a word that is hated. There are a lot of words in the Bible that are hated—words like *blood*, and *redemption*, and *the Cross*. Paul says the Cross is an offense, but that cannot keep us from preaching about it. The Bible teaches dispensations, and so we will not avoid the subject at all.

Let me say first of all that a dispensation is not a period of time. That is where *dispensation* differs from the word *age*. We hear of the "age of grace"—that is a period of time. *Dispensation* is an altogether different word that is translated in several different ways. It can mean "a stewardship," "an order," or "an administration." An English transliteration of the Greek word would be "economy." It is an order or a system that is put into effect; it is the way of doing things.

For example, girls in school take a course called home economics or domestic economy. They learn how to run a household. When a woman has her own home, she may decide to have baked beans one night and a roast the next night. She sets up the order of meals and that is the way she organizes her schedule. Down the street the mother in another family decides they won't have a roast that night, but they will have fish. That is the way she runs her house, and she has a right to run it like that. There is also a political economy—a subject that is taught in our colleges today. A lot of young men go into that field, and they learn how to run the government, the way to run a nation. England runs her government differently from the way we do in the United States. Each has a right to its own system and I wouldn't say that either place has the right system. Russia has an entirely different system; we certainly wouldn't better ours by taking theirs. Countries even have different systems of running traffic. In England they drive down the left side of the street. I enjoyed kidding our driver when we were in England, "Look out, there comes a car on the wrong side of the street!" "That's all right," he would say, "I'm going on the wrong side myself." In England, the right side is the left side. Now that is confusing to a poor American visiting over there.

A dispensation *may* fit into a certain period of time, but it actually means the way God runs something at a particular time: it is the way God does things. It is evident that God had Adam on a different arrangement than He has for you and me. I think even the most ardent antidispensationalist can understand that the Garden of Eden was different from Southern California today. And God dealt with Adam in a different way than He deals with us. (Now, I will admit that when people first moved out to Southern California, they thought it was the Garden of Eden. I thought so, too, when I first came here, but now it is filled with smog and traffic!)

Now God has never had but one method of saving folk; everything rests upon one method of salvation. The approach and the man under the system have been different, however. For example, Abel offered a lamb to God, and so did Abraham. The Old Testament priests offered lambs to God. God had said that was the right way. But I hope you didn't bring a lamb to church last Sunday! That is not the way God tells us to approach Him today. We are under a different economy.

"Of the fulness of times." What is the "fulness of times"? I can't go into all phases of that, but God is moving everything forward to the time when Christ will rule over all things in heaven and earth. This is the fullness, the *pleroma,* when everything is going to be brought under the rulership of Jesus Christ. The *pleroma* is like a vast receptacle into which centuries and millenniums have been falling. All that is past, present, and future is moving toward the time when every knee must bow and every tongue must confess that Jesus is Lord. This is the mystery that is revealed to us, "That in the dispensation of the fulness of times he might gather together in one all things in Christ, both which are in heaven, and which are on earth; even in him." We learn this about Christ, that God ". . . hast put all things in subjection under his feet. For in that he put all in subjection under him, he left nothing that is not put under him. But now we see not yet all things put under him" (Heb. 2:8). This states very clearly that we have not yet come to that time. We are under a different dispensation today; we live under a different economy. But God has revealed this to us that is to come to pass, something that had not been revealed in the past.

Heaven and earth are not in tune today—we are playing our own little tune. We have our rock music going down here, while the only Rock up there is the Lord Jesus. He is *the* Rock. He is that precious Stone that is the foundation upon which the church rests today. And the day will come when heaven and earth will be in tune and all things will be gathered together in Christ.

Now we come to the third work of God the Son on behalf of the church: Christ rewards us with an inheritance.

In whom also we have obtained an inheritance, being predestinated according to the purpose of him who worketh all things after the counsel of his own will:

That we should be to the praise of his glory, who first trusted in Christ [Eph. 1:11–12].

Here is another marvelous truth. He gives us an inheritance—He rewards us for something we have not done. It is the overall purpose and plan of God that believers should have a part in Christ's inheritance. They are going to inherit with Christ because they are in Christ. Paul writes, "And if children, then heirs; heirs of God, and joint-heirs with Christ; if so be that we suffer with him, that we may be also glorified together" (Rom. 8:17). "Therefore let no man glory in men. For all things are yours; whether Paul, or Apollos, or Cephas, or the world, or life, or death, or things present, or things to come; all are yours; and ye are Christ's; and Christ is God's" (1 Cor 3:21–23). I really don't grasp at all this tremendous statement God makes to us, but it causes me to be lifted from the seat in which I'm sitting and carries me right into the sky. Everything is mine! Christ belongs to me. Paul belongs to me. Even death may belong to me. *All* is mine. It is mine because He has given it to me. Christ is mine. God is mine. What an experience for us!

I feel like shouting because this is so wonderful. God has predestinated this; He has determined it. This refers to the saved—remember that God never predestinated anybody to be lost. He predestinated us to receive an inheritance. If He hadn't predestinated it to me, I would never get one. It is something I do not deserve. It is a reward out of His grace and not out of my merit. This is God's will, and that is the only basis on which it is done. It is good, and it is right, and it is the best. Why? Because God has purposed it. You just can't have it any better than that.

Oh, these are the three marvelous things Christ has done for us: He's redeemed us with His blood; He's revealed the mystery of His will; and He rewards us with an inheritance. How wonderful it is—I can't lose! He paid for the church, and I belong to Him because He paid a price.

May I say that the church is very important to Him today. The little plans of men down here—they're not important. We think they are. Men are running around with a blueprint for the world today, but they won't even be around here in the next one hundred years—that crowd will all be gone. But God's great plans *will* be carried out. Thank God for that!

Verse twelve is one of those glorious doxologies that we find throughout the epistles. You will notice that Paul stops and "sings" the doxology after he tells what each person of the Godhead has done. He has just finished telling us about the work of the Son. Then he writes, "That we should be to the praise of his glory, who first trusted in Christ." God does not exist to satisfy the whim and wish of the believer. The believer exists for the glory of God. When the believer is in the center of the will of God, he is living a life of fullness and of satisfaction and of joy. That will deliver you from the hands of psychologists, friend. But when you are not in the will of God, there is trouble brewing for you. Living in God's will adds purpose and meaning to life: we are going to be for the praise of His glory. God will be able throughout the endless ages of eternity future to point to you and me and say, "Look there, they weren't worth saving but I loved them and I saved them." That is the thing which gives worth and standing and dignity and purpose and joy and glory to life. We exist today to the praise of His glory and that is enough.

This doxology looks forward, of course, to the coming of Christ. The third doxology, we shall see, concerns the work of the Holy Spirit.

GOD THE HOLY SPIRIT PROTECTS THE CHURCH

When we look at the work of the Holy Spirit, we see that (1) He regenerates us, (2) He is a refuge for us, and (3) He gives reality to our lives. We come first to regeneration.

> **In whom ye also trusted, after that ye heard the word of truth, the gospel of your salvation: in whom also after that ye believed, ye were sealed with that holy Spirit of promise [Eph. 1:13].**

This section, I believe, is one of the most wonderful in Scripture. "Well," somebody says, "he doesn't mention regeneration here." Actually he does, and in a marvelous way, because now we're passing from God's work *for us* to the work of the Holy Spirit *in us.* The work of God in planning the church and the work of the Lord Jesus in redeeming the church and paying for it were objective. The work of the Holy Spirit in protecting the church is different because it is subjective; it is *in us.*

In this work of regeneration and renewing, the Holy Spirit causes the sinner to hear and believe in his heart, and that makes him a child of God. The Lord Jesus said, ". . . Ye must be born again" (John 3:7). How are we to be born again? John explains, "But as many as received him, to them gave he power to become the sons of God, even to them that believe on his name" (John 1:12). We need simply to believe on His name.

"In whom ye also trusted, after that ye heard the word of truth." Hearing means to hear not just the sound of words but to hear with understanding. Paul wrote, "But we preach Christ crucified, unto the Jews a stumblingblock, and unto the Greeks foolishness; but unto them which are called, both Jews and Greeks, Christ the power of God, and the wisdom of God" (1 Cor. 1:23–24). Who are the called? Are they the ones that just heard the sound of words? No, it means those who heard with understanding. God called them. It was not just a call of hearing words, but a call where the Holy Spirit made those words real. Faith comes by hearing, and hearing by the Word of God, according to Romans 10:17. Those who are called hear the Word of God and they respond to it. Then what happens? Peter puts it this way: "Being born again, not of corruptible seed, but of incorruptible, by the word of God, which liveth and abideth for ever" (1 Pet. 1:23). The Word of God goes out as it is going out even through this printed page. We are saying that the Son of God died for you and if you trust Him, you will be saved. "Well," someone may say, "I read these words, but they mean nothing to me." Someone else, however, will read or hear this message, and the Spirit of God will apply it to his heart so that he believes—he trusts—and the moment he trusts in Christ, he is regenerated. Believing is the logical step after hearing. It may not be the next chronological step, but it is the logical step. "In whom ye also trusted, after that ye heard the word of truth." This is the best explanation of what it means to be born again that I know of in the Word of God. You hear the Word of Truth—the gospel of your salvation, the good news of your deliverance—and you put your trust in Christ.

"In whom also after that ye believed, ye were sealed with that holy Spirit of promise." I would like to remove the word *after* from this verse because these are not time clauses. They are what is known in the Greek as genitive absolutes, and they are all the same tense as the main verb. It means that when you heard and you believed, you were also sealed: it all took place at the same time. A truer translation would be, "In whom also you, upon hearing [aorist tense] the word of truth, the good news of your salvation, in whom also on believing [aorist tense] you were sealed with the Holy Spirit of promise." This is, by the way, when the baptism of the Holy Spirit occurs. You are baptized the moment that you trust Christ. You are also sealed the moment that you trust Christ. The Holy Spirit first opens the ear to hear, and then He implants faith. His next logical step, you see, is to seal the believer.

There are people today who argue whether God the Father or God the Son seals with the Holy Spirit, or whether the Holy Spirit Himself does the sealing. That type of argument wearies me. They tried to split hairs in that way in the Middle Ages and would argue how many angels could dance on the point of a needle. You toss that around for a little while, and it will get you nowhere. I understand this verse to mean that the Holy Spirit is the seal. God the Father gave the Son to die on the cross, but the Son offered up Himself willingly. So both the Father and the Son gave. God the Father and God the Son both sent the Holy Spirit to perform a definite work, but it is the Spirit who does the work. He regenerates the sinner and He seals the sinner at the same time, and I think that the Spirit Himself is that seal.

There is a twofold purpose in the sealing work of the Holy Spirit. He implants the image of God upon the heart to give reality to the believer. You know that a seal is put down on a document and that seal has an image on it. I think that is exactly what the Spirit of God does to the believer. "He that hath received his testimony hath set to his seal that God is true" (John 3:33). Apparently, this is the thought here—God has put His implant upon the believer.

The second purpose of the sealing is to denote rightful ownership. "Nevertheless the foundation of God standeth sure, having this seal, the Lord knoweth them that are his. And, let every one that nameth the name of Christ depart from iniquity" (2 Tim. 2:19). The fact that He makes you secure does not mean that you can live in sin. If you name the name of Christ, you are going to depart from iniquity. If there is not this evidence, then you were not regenerated or sealed.

The Holy Spirit is the seal, and that guarantees that God is going to deliver us. We are sealed until the day of redemption. The day will come when the Holy Spirit will deliver us to Christ. It's nice to be sealed like that—we are just like a letter that is insured. In the old days they would put a seal on it. Today they just stamp it with a special stamp, but it still means that the post office guarantees to deliver that letter.

Now we come to the third and final work of the Holy Spirit in protecting the church.

Which is the earnest of our inheritance until the redemption of the purchased possession, unto the praise of his glory [Eph. 1:14].

Earnest money is the money that is put forth as a down payment and pledge on a piece of property. It means you want them to hold the property for you. It also means that you promise there is more money to follow. The Holy Spirit is our earnest money. He has been given as a pledge and token that there is more to follow in the way of spiritual blessings. We have already seen that we have an inheritance—there is more to follow. The Holy Spirit is that earnest, that guarantee.

All of this is to "the praise of his glory." This is now the third doxology in this chapter. As we have seen, Paul gives a doxology after he considers the work of each member of the Trinity. Here it is to the praise of the glory of God that the Holy Spirit regenerates us, becomes our refuge and seal, and gives us reality. All these glorious truths now move Paul to prayer.

PRAYER OF PAUL FOR KNOWLEDGE AND POWER FOR THE EPHESIANS

Wherefore I also, after I heard of your faith in the Lord Jesus, and love unto all the saints,

Cease not to give thanks for you, making mention of you in my prayers [Eph. 1:15–16].

The Ephesian church was noted for its faith and love. Love wasn't just a motto, not just a bumper sticker, for these people. There was real love expressed by the saints. It was based on their faith in the Lord Jesus. This was the church at its highest. In the Book of Revelation the Ephesian church represents the early church at its very best. Because of their faith and love, Paul thanks God for the Ephesians.

It seems that the circumstances that motivate us to pray are trouble, sickness, distress, or a crisis. People asked me to pray for a church recently because it was in trouble: there was no love for the brethren, it was filled with gossip, and Bible study no longer held the highest priority. I love this church and I do pray for them, but it is sad that there are so many negative things that always seem to motivate us to pray. Paul was often motivated by the good things. When you hear something good about a child of God, are you motivated to say, "Oh God, I thank You for this brother and the way You are using him"? When you hear of a wonderful Bible church where God is blessing the preacher, and the Word of God is going out, do you get down on your knees and thank God for it? My friend, isn't it true that too often we turn in a kind of grocery list to God? "I want this, I want that, I want the other thing." "Lord, will You do this, will You do that?" God is not a messenger boy. Why don't we thank Him sometimes? We need more thanksgiving services. I think He would appreciate all of us having a time of thanksgiving regularly—not just once a year.

A preacher friend of mine told me that their prayer meeting got so stale and so dull and so small that they tried something new. They decided that at the prayer meeting they would do nothing but praise God and thank Him. He declared, "We sure had some brief prayers, but we had a good prayer meeting that night. Nobody asked God for anything. They just thanked Him for what He had done."

Paul says, when he heard the good news and wonderful reports about the Ephesian church, "I . . . cease not to give thanks for you." It's interesting that we don't too often think of Paul as an outstanding man of prayer. We would put him at the top of the list as a great missionary of the cross. We can't think of any greater example of apostleship than Paul. If you were to make a list of ten of the greatest preachers of the church, you would certainly put Paul as number one. He was also one of the greatest teachers. The Lord Jesus was, of course, the greatest of all—". . . Never man spake like this man" (John 7:46)—and Paul certainly followed in that tradition. He is also an example of a good pastor. According to Dr. Luke, Paul wept with the believers at Ephesus when he took leave of them. He loved them, and they loved him.

I always judge the spiritual life of a church by the way they love their pastor, providing he stands for the Word of God. One can pretty well judge the attitude of the people by the way they love their pastor. Today we need to judge folk by their attitude toward the Word of God rather than how big a Bible they carry under their arms. The Ephesians not only loved Paul, but they loved God's Word.

When you think of anyone excelling in any field of service in the early church, Paul the apostle must be up toward the top. How about being representative of a great man of prayer—would you put Paul in that list? We think of Moses as the great intercessor on the top of the mountain. We think of David with his psalms and his confession of his awful sin. We think of Elijah who stood alone before an altar drenched with water at Mount Carmel. Then there was Daniel who opened his window toward Jerusalem and prayed even though he lived in a hostile land under a hostile power. The Lord Jesus was the Man of prayer, so much so that one of His disciples asked Him, ". . . Lord, teach us to pray . . ." (Luke 11:1). Did you know that Paul was also a great man of prayer? When I was teaching in the Bible Institute of Los Angeles, I would ask the students during their study of the epistles of Paul to make a list of all the prayers of the apostle Paul. They were to put down every time he said he was praying for someone. Lo and behold, student after student would come to me and say, "I had no idea that Paul had such a prayer list. I didn't know he prayed for so many people!" Paul was a great man of prayer.

There are two of the prayers of Paul in this epistle. We are looking at the first one. Having set before us the children of Israel as the body of Christ, Paul falls to his knees and begins to pray. The other prayer is at the end of the third chapter. These two prayers in this epistle indicate Paul's concern as a child of God for other believers. One of the ways one can judge whether or not a person is a child of God is by his prayer life. How much does he feel a dependence on God? If he has a need, he will go to God in prayer for himself. He will also go to God in intercession for others. Many people who have written from all over this country, and from other countries as well, have told me when I've met them, "I remember you in prayer." Well, that to me is an indication of their faith. Remember that Ananias in the city of Damascus was disturbed when the angel told him to go to Saul of Tarsus. He objected because Saul was the man who was persecuting the church, but the angel said to him, ". . . behold, he prayeth" (Acts 9:11). That was an indication to Ananias the something had happened to Saul of Tarsus.

"Cease not to give thanks for you." Paul first of all gives thanks to God for the Ephesians. They were on his prayer list, and I guess all the churches were.

"Making mention of you in my prayers." That means he called them all by name. I was with a great preacher one time, and some folk came up and spoke to him and shook hands with us. One man said to him, "I'm praying for you." I shall never forget what the preacher asked him, "Thank you very much, but do you mention me by name? I don't want the Lord to get me mixed up with somebody else." Call people by name when you pray for them.

We have seen that the motive for Paul's prayer was good news. Now we will see that he does not pray for material things but for spiritual blessings. These are the blessings that are all-important.

That the God of our Lord Jesus Christ, the Father of glory, may give unto you the spirit of wisdom and revelation in the knowledge of him [Eph. 1:17].

Paul, having written that the church is the body of Christ, and that God the Father planned it, God the Son paid for it, and God the Holy Spirit protects it, recognized that the Ephesians wouldn't be able to understand all this unless the Spirit of God was their teacher and opened the Word of God to them. Only the Holy Spirit of God could reveal the knowledge of God.

When Dr. H. A. Ironside lived in Southern California as a young man and was preaching in this area, he would sometimes visit a wonderful man of God who had come from Northern Ireland because of his health. This man had what was called in those days "galloping consumption," and he was living his last days in a little tent out back of the home of Dr. Ironside's parents. He had been greatly used of God in teaching the Word. While Dr. Ironside would sit with him, he would open up the Scriptures in such an amazing way that Dr. Ironside one day asked him, "Where did you learn that?" "Well," this man said, "I didn't get it by going to seminary because I never went to seminary. I never learned it by going to college. No one particularly taught me. Rather I learned these things on my knees on the mud floor of a little sod cottage in the north of Ireland. There with my open Bible before me, I used to kneel for hours at a time and ask the Spirit of God to reveal Christ to my soul, and open the Word to my heart. He taught me more on my knees on that mud floor than I could have learned in all the seminaries and colleges of the world."

Having known Dr. Ironside personally, I can say that he too practiced a dependence on the Holy Spirit in his own ministry. I remember when he was teaching us the Song of Solomon, he said that he was never satisfied with what he found in the commentaries, and he just got down on his knees and asked God to reveal to him the message of that book. Well, he wrote a commentary on the Song of Solomon and, very frankly, his interpretation of it is the only one that has ever satisfied my own heart.

What a wonderful, glorious thing it is to have the Spirit of God be the One to teach us. "That the God of our Lord Jesus Christ . . . may give unto you the spirit of wisdom and revelation in the knowledge of him." How will that take place? It will take place by the Spirit of God—the only One who can open our eyes—teaching us God's Word.

The eyes of your understanding being enlightened; that ye may know what is the hope of his calling, and what the riches of the glory of his inheritance in the saints [Eph. 1:18].

More literally it reads, "the eyes of your heart being enlightened." It is not the eyes of your mind but the eyes of your heart that must understand. One can be very brilliant intellectually, but that is no guarantee that there will be an understanding of spiritual truth. Scripture puts more emphasis on the understanding of the heart than of the head. Paul writes, "That if thou shalt confess with thy mouth the Lord Jesus, and shalt believe in thine heart that God hath raised him from the dead, thou shalt be saved. For with the heart man believeth unto righteousness; and with the mouth confession is made unto salvation" (Rom. 10:9–10).

I have no understanding of music whatsoever. I can't sing and I can't carry a tune. I recognize very few tunes, and I do not know what a pitch is. It is all a foreign field to me. One time a music director made the statement publicly that he could teach anybody to sing. I stood up immediately and said, "Brother, you have a pupil. Nobody has ever been able to teach me to sing." The congregation laughed, and we made an engagement. I met with him every Thursday afternoon for a month, and at the end of the month he gave up. He said, "I believe you are right. You'll never be able to learn music." I asked, "How could I ever learn?" He said, "The only way in the world would be for you to be born again." He didn't mean spiritually; he meant born another person. My friend, as far as spiritual knowledge is concerned, no person can understand it apart from the Spirit of God. This is what we are told in 1 Corinthians 2:9–10: "But as it is written, Eye hath not seen, nor ear heard, neither have entered into the heart of man, the things which God hath prepared for them that love him. But

God hath revealed them unto us by his Spirit: for the Spirit searcheth all things, yea, the deep things of God."

I knew a dear lady in Sherman, Texas. We all called her "Grandma," and she was a wonderful lady, but she could neither read nor write. I was just a first-year seminary student and I thought I had the answer to everything, so I went to visit her. I started out by trying to explain John 14 to her. I thought I'd make it simple for Grandma. She listened about five minutes and then said, "Young man, have you ever noticed this in that chapter?"—and then she went on to point out something from that Scripture. Well, to be honest, I hadn't noticed it. I couldn't understand how she could have such insight when she couldn't read or write. She knew things I couldn't find in the commentaries. How did she know? The eyes of her heart were opened by the Spirit of God.

The Spirit of God wants to teach us today. One of the reasons that God's people are not in the Word of God is because they are not willing for the Spirit of God to teach them. They depend on a poor preacher like me or on a home Bible class. These all have their place but, Christian friend, why don't you let the Spirit of God teach you? Spend time in the Scriptures. When you come to a particular passage of Scripture, you may think it to be a barren place. If you don't understand it and you read it many times and don't seem to see much of anything in it, then get down on your knees before the Lord and say to the Lord, "I missed the point and You will have to teach me." This is what I do. He teaches me, and I know He will teach you.

"That ye may know what is the hope of his calling, and what the riches of the glory of his inheritance in the saints." We have learned that we have an inheritance in the Lord. We are also to know that He has an inheritance in us. I think an illustration of this would be the land of Canaan. The land belonged to God, but He gave it to the children of Israel as their possession. The children of Israel are tied into that land; yet the day will come when God will take possession of this entire universe and will reclaim Israel as well as the land as His own. Today you and I, as believers, are His church and God operates through us, but the time is coming when we shall rule and reign with Him. He will claim us as *His* inheritance. I have wondered about that—this is an area that is just too deep for me to apprehend. I need the Spirit of God to make this real to me.

Paul continues his petition:

> **And what is the exceeding greatness of his power to usward who believe, according to the working of his mighty power [Eph. 1:19].**

Let me amplify this: What is the exceeding (intense) greatness of His power (*dunameos*—dynamite power) to usward who believe, according to the working (*energeian*—the energizing) of the strength of His might.

How great is that dynamite power, that energizing strength?

> **Which he wrought in Christ, when he raised him from the dead, and set him at his own right hand in the heavenly places [Eph. 1:20].**

It is power enough to raise Christ from the dead—a tremendous power. Not only is it resurrection power, but it is the power that set Christ at God's right hand, and that is ascension power. We don't make much of the Ascension in our Bible churches today; we emphasize Christmas and Easter, but we seem to forget the events after that. Have you ever stopped to think of the power that took Him back to the right hand of God? That, my friend, is power. We are beginning to see a little of it. Think of the power it takes to lift a missile off its base and take it out into space, and the power it took to take men to the moon and bring them back. That is power in the physical realm. The power that took Christ to the right hand of God is the same power that is available to believers today. That is why Paul prays that believers may know the greatness of that power. He writes, "That I may know him, and the power of his resurrection . . ." (Phil. 3:10).

> **Far above all principality, and power, and might, and dominion, and every name that is named, not only in this world, but also in that which is to come:**

> **And hath put all things under his feet, and gave him to be the head over all things to the church,**
>
> **Which is his body, the fulness of him that filleth all in all [Eph. 1:21–23].**

Paul concludes on a tremendously high note. The church is the body of Christ, and Christ is the Head of the church. Someday everything is going to be under Him. The writer to the Hebrews makes it clear, "Thou hast put all things in subjection under his feet. For in that he put all in subjection under him, he left nothing that is not put under him. But now we see not yet all things put under him" (Heb. 2:8).

At the present time the only thing that is under Him is the church. By this I mean the true church, the real believers. There are many organized groups who call themselves churches who are not listening to the Lord Jesus. These churches are paralyzed. You see, the most tragic sight is a child of God lying on a bed, helpless, as if his brain is detached from his body. I've been in many churches that have been like that and there are many individual Christians today who act as if they are detached from Christ, the Head of the body. He says, "If ye love me, keep my commandments" (John 14:15). In other words, I can wiggle my little finger because my head is in charge of it; and when He wants you to "wiggle"—that is, exercise whatever gift He has given you—down here, you do it because of love, or else you're not attached to Him. How important this is today! Paul pictures the church and our relationship to it in this way: "For as the body is one, and hath many members, and all the members of that one body, being many, are one body: so also is Christ. For by one Spirit are we all baptized into one body, whether we be Jews or Gentiles, whether we be bond or free; and have been all made to drink into one Spirit" (1 Cor. 12:12–13). The thing we need to see is that Christ is the Head of the body, His church, and we are under Him.

CHAPTER 2

THEME: *The church is a temple; the material for temple construction; the method of construction; the meaning of the construction*

This chapter begins with the little conjuction *and;* so it is actually a continuation of the thought of the first chapter. Paul has been talking about that tremendous power that raised Jesus from the dead. We shall see that this power is the same power that made us, when we were dead in trespasses and sins, alive in Christ. That takes power! It takes *resurrection* power. It is this power that so many of God's children want to experience. Frances Ridley Havergal expresses it in as lovely and fine a way as it could be, and I'm sure it is a prayer in the hearts of many Christians today.

> Oh, let me know
> The power of the resurrection;
> Oh, let me show
> Thy risen life in calm and clear reflection;
> Oh, let me give
> Out of the gifts thou freely gavest;
> Oh, let me live
> With life abundantly because thou livest.
> —Frances Ridley Havergal

Now it seems that God is rather reluctant about letting man have power. I think we can see why. God let centuries go by with man knowing nothing of atomic power. Then man discovered atomic power, and it changed the world. What did it do to the world? Did it make it a wonderful place in which to live? You know that it made the world a frightful place in which to live because it gave man the power to destroy the world. Man is dangerous today. We live like an ostrich with our head in the sand if we think to ourselves that no nation dares to release that atomic power. There are men in positions of power today who would turn it loose tomorrow, or even today, if they thought they could get by with it. Man is dangerous with the use of physical power. I think God is reluctant to give man power.

However, the power of God which the epistle speaks of is the power that God will release in the life of one who will turn to Jesus Christ. He will lift that person out of spiritual death into spiritual life. This power will be exhibited by Christ in the world. The Lord Jesus expresses Himself in the world today through His church.

In many ways the church as a temple corresponds to the temple of the Old Testament which was, in turn, preceded by the tabernacle of the wilderness. The comparison is self-evident. The contrasts are sharp and striking. The tabernacle and the temple, for instance, were made of living trees of acacia wood that were hewn into dead boards. In order to form the church, God takes dead material and makes it into a living temple. The temple and tabernacle were dwelling places for the glory of God. The church is a dwelling place for the person of the Holy Spirit. The tabernacle and temple were for the performance of a ritual and the repetition of a sacrifice for sin. The church is built upon the one sacrifice of Christ in the historical past, a sacrifice which is not repeated. "Nor yet that he should offer himself often, as the high priest entereth into the holy place every year with blood of others; for then must he often have suffered since the foundation of the world: but now once in the end of the world hath he appeared to put away sin by the sacrifice of himself" (Heb. 9:25–26). Nor does the church have a ritual. It is a functional organism in which the Holy Spirit moves through the living stones.

Let me emphasize here that God has not given a ritual to the church as there was a ritual in the temple. Some folk think that they have had a church service by opening with the doxology, saying a prayer, singing hymns, and then sitting down to listen to the Scripture being expounded. Yet to them it was only a meaningless ritual— and the church has not been given a ritual. Someone may ask, "Then we're not to do that?" Well, the point is that just going through the exercise of mouthing words has become a meaningless ritual to a lot of folk today. These things should have *meaning*. They are proper, of course, when meaning is expressed.

Now the church is not only minus a temple ritual; it is also not a temple "made with hands." The impressive fact of the church age is that God is indwelling individual believers. Notice the following verses: "God that made the world and all things therein, seeing that he is Lord of heaven and earth, dwelleth not in temples made with hands; neither is worshipped with men's hands, as though he needed any thing, seeing he giveth to all life, and breath, and all things" (Acts 17:24–25). "What? know ye not that your body is the temple of the Holy Ghost which is in you, which ye have of God, and ye are not your own? For ye are bought with a price: therefore glorify God in your body, and in your spirit, which are God's" (1 Cor. 6:19–20).

I want to emphasize here that Israel never did believe that God was confined to the temple. When Solomon was dedicating the temple, he prayed, "But will God indeed dwell on the earth? behold, the heaven and heaven of heavens cannot contain thee; how much less this house that I have builded?" (1 Kings 8:27). Every instructed Israelite understood that God did not live in a temple—a little box. The liberals try to give the impression that they had such a conception. I heard a Vanderbilt University professor say that the Israelites had a primitive viewpoint of God; they thought He could dwell in a little box. I'd like to say that the professor had a primitive view of the Bible. If he had just read his Old Testament, he would have known that Israel did not believe that. God had told them that the temple was the place where He would meet with them. That is why they came to the temple with a sacrifice and a ritual. The church has none of that today.

Another sharp contrast to the Old Testament temple is the position of the Gentiles. You will recall that the Gentiles had to come as proselytes and were confined to the court of the Gentiles. In Jerusalem today at the Holy City Hotel is a replica of the city of Jerusalem as it looked in the days of Herod, which were, of course, the days of Christ. The court of the Gentiles was way off to the left as you look into the temple. The Gentiles didn't get very close. That is why Paul says in this chapter, "But now in Christ Jesus ye who sometimes were far off are made nigh by the blood of Christ" (v. 13). You see, we who are Gentiles have been brought in pretty close. In fact, we are seated in the heavenlies in Christ! You just can't improve on that.

THE MATERIAL FOR TEMPLE CONSTRUCTION

And you hath he quickened, who were dead in trespasses and sins;

Wherein in time past ye walked according to the course of this world, according to the prince of the power of the air, the spirit that now worketh in the children of disobedience [Eph. 2:1–2].

Now let me quote my own translation of these verses. (My translation is published only in my book, *Exploring Through Ephesians*. I have made no attempt to produce a polished translation. I simply pull the original Greek words over into English so that you might be able to get a little different viewpoint. I have done this for years—in Southern California it is known as *The McGee-icus Ad Absurdum Translation*.) Now here is a literal translation of the verse: And you being dead in your trespasses and sins, in which you once walked according to age (spirit of the age, secularism, course, principle) of this world (cosmos, society, civilization), according to the prince of the power (authority) of the air (haze, smog), of the spirit that now worketh (energizes) in the sons (children) of disobedience.

"And you being dead in your trespasses and sins." Perhaps you notice that I left out "hath he quickened," which in your Bible is printed in italics. This means it was not in the original text but was inserted to smooth out the translation. I am perfectly willing to admit that something belongs there to give explanation, and "hath he quickened" is all right, but I am trying to pull out the original and give you the meaning without smoothing out the translation.

"You being dead in your trespasses and sins in which you once walked according to the age"—the spirit of the age. That is, according to secularism, according to the way of the world, or according to the principle of this world. The "world" does not mean the physical universe. It means the cosmos, society, civilization, life-pattern, or lifestyle of the world today.

"According to the prince of the power [authority] of the air, the spirit that now worketh (that is, energizes) in the children [sons] of disobedience." The devil takes this dead material (we are dead in trespasses and sins) and he energizes us. That is the reason the cults are as busy as termites, and with the same results. False religionists put us to shame in their zeal. Satan is energizing them. People ask me whether I am aware that miracles are being performed in the cults. I won't argue that. Maybe they are. I know some things are exaggerated in our day, but maybe some of them are true. Then who is doing the miracles? Satan is able to duplicate a great many of the miracles that are scriptural miracles. After all, weren't the magicians of Egypt able to duplicate the first miracles performed by Moses? Of course the later miracles they could not duplicate. When man gets into the realm of the new birth and closeness to God, Satan is powerless against him, but he is potent today to delude and to deceive and to lead people astray. He is potent today in the cults and false "isms" of the world.

Among whom also we all had our conversation in times past in the lusts of our flesh, fulfilling the desires of the flesh and of the mind; and were by nature the children of wrath, even as others [Eph. 2:3].

To better understand verses 1–7, we need to recognize that they comprise a single periodic sentence in the Greek language. Classical Greek is filled with periodic sentences, all kinds of genitive absolutes, phrases, and tenses—it is difficult to read. Koine Greek is generally easy to read, but here is a periodic sentence which reveals that Paul was capable of writing better Greek than the Koine of his day. The Authorized Version, by the way, breaks this into a sentence that ends at verse three. That is permissible and entirely right because verse four is a contrasting statement joined by the conjunction *but*.

We have already noted that the chapter begins with *and*, which connects it to the preceding chapter. In chapter 1 Paul had been talking about salvation and picked up the theme of the mighty greatness of His power in verse 19. This is the power that quickens dead sinners. Now here in chapter 2, verse 1, he says that we were dead in trespasses and sins. That speaks to the death of Adam which is imputed to us. "Wherefore, as by one man sin entered into the world, and death by sin; and so death passed upon all men, for that all have sinned" (Rom. 5:12). Adam's sin made us the sons of a fallen man, and we all have the same nature that Adam had. It is a fallen nature with no capacity or inclination to God.

When I look back upon my own conversion, I really think it was a miracle. How in the world could God save a boy who had been brought up as I had been? My father had high moral principles and was known as an honest man, but he was not a Christian and was antagonistic to the church. He never darkened the door of a church, but he made me go to Sunday school as a boy—and I always protested against going. Then my dad died when I was fourteen, and I found myself adrift in the world. I ran all the way to Detroit, Michigan, to get away from every authority. I turned down work for Ford Motor Company and took a job with Cadillac. There I got into awful sin. I associated with a group of men, particularly a man from Hungary who thought I looked like his son who had died. He took me under his wing. But he was a sinful man and took me places where a sixteen-year-old boy ought not to go. I got homesick and went back home, and when I think back to it now, I realize that it was God who made me homesick. If I hadn't gone back home, the devil would have won the day. I was dead to God and to the things of God. Then a man told me I could have peace with God through Jesus Christ. How wonderful that was! I say it was a miracle. I wasn't looking for God. I was running from Him as fast as I could because I was dead in trespasses and sins.

Adam died spiritually the day he disbelieved and disobeyed God. He ran away from God and tried to hide. He wasn't looking for God. That is the position of natural man today. This idea that men have a little spark of the divine and are looking for God is as false as can be. On the day Adam disobeyed, he died to God and to the things of God, although he didn't die physically until nine hundred years after he had eaten the fruit. But he had lost his capacity and longing for God. He was separated from God. After all, death is separation. All death is a separation. Physical death is separation of the spirit and the soul from the body. When someone dies, we don't see the separation of the spirit and the soul; we see only the dead body. Spiritual death is a separation from God. After man sinned, he could go on living physically and mentally, but he was spiritually dead, separated from God. He passed that same dead nature on to all his offspring. It is only the convicting work of the Holy Spirit that can prick the conscience of any man in this world today. You can't do it and I can't do it. Only the Spirit of God can do it.

I had the privilege of being pastor of a great church in downtown Los Angeles. I followed great preachers including the first pastor of that church, Dr. R. A. Torrey. I wanted to do a creditable job, and I wanted to bring glory to God. I would always pray as I left the radio room to go to the pulpit platform to preach, "Lord God, I recognize that I am helpless and hopeless. I will be speaking into a graveyard— many sitting out here are dead in trespasses and sins. Oh God, I can be powerful if the Spirit of God will move." Only the Spirit of God can speak so that dead men will hear. Thank God, the Spirit of God did move and continues to move so that dead men are able to hear! The Lord Jesus told His disciples that He would send the Comforter to them, "And when he is come, he will reprove [convict] the world of sin, and of righteousness, and of judgment" (John 16:8). Do you know that you and I who live in this world are living in a cemetery? Men are dead.

A famous judge traveled around this country years ago giving a lecture entitled: "Millions Now Living Will Never Die." A great preacher followed him on his speaking circuit with this message. "Millions Now Living Are Already Dead." He was more accurate than the judge had been. Millions, actually billions, are dead in trespasses and sins.

An old Irishman was asked to define a cemetery. He said, "A cemetery is a place where the dead live." That describes our world.

A trespass is what Adam did. He stepped over God's bounds. Sin means to miss the mark. We just don't come up to God's standard at all. That is our condition: dead in trespasses and sins and energized by Satan. That is the description of us before we are saved, and every unsaved man is walking around in this world like a spiritual zombie.

The description of our past is not very pretty. We walked according to the spirit of the age. We conformed to the society and the civilization and the life-style of the world. We were walking according to the prince of the power of the air, the spirit that energizes the sons of disobedience. That is Satan and he takes folks and leads them around.

Today, when Christians talk about being separated from the world, they think of that which is fleshly or carnal or godless. The characteristic sins of the lost world are the mental and spiritual sins; and these are, actually, I think, in God's sight, worse than the physical sins.

Listen to James 4:1-4: "From whence come wars and fightings among you? come they not hence, even of your lusts that war in your members? Ye lust, and have not: ye kill, and desire to have, and cannot obtain: ye fight and war, yet ye have not, because ye ask not. Ye ask, and receive not, because ye ask amiss, that ye may consume it upon your lusts. Ye adulterers and adulteresses, know ye not that the friendship of the world is enmity with God? whosoever therefore will be a friend of the world is the enemy of God."

A great many folk come to church on Sunday, pious as a church mouse (however pious that may be), and think they are separated from the world. On Monday morning they start out in this rough, workaday world just as mean and hard and after the almighty dollar as everyone else. They want it to consume it on their own selves, for their own selfish desires. That is what James is talking about. The believer has been saved from that.

John puts it in these words: "Love not the world, neither the things that are in the world. If any man love the world, the love of the Father is not in him. For all that is in the world, the lust of the flesh, and the lust of the eyes, and the pride of life, is not of the Father, but is of the world. And the world passeth away, and the lust thereof: but he that doeth the will of God abideth for ever" (1 John 2:15-17).

There are a great many people today who say they do not live in gross sin. They say, "No, I would not commit these sins. I wouldn't live and act like certain people do." Dr. G. Campbell Morgan used to ask the question, "Would you *like* to live as they do?" Do you like to watch people sinning on the TV screen because that way you do those same things vicariously? I've always felt that the reason the story of the prodigal son is so popular with some is because of the way it is sometimes preached. You notice that the Lord Jesus never mentioned any of the sins that boy committed when he was in the far country, but I've heard sermons in which you were taken along with him from one night club to another, from one barroom to another, from one brothel to another. Some saints really enjoyed those sermons because they could enjoy the sin vicariously. That's what John is talking about when he says love not the world. Do you really love it? How do you feel about it?

I remember when Mrs. McGee and I first came to California. We were just fresh out of Texas. In fact, I had never seen a body of water that I couldn't throw a stone across. We were amazed at the ocean. We drove from San Diego to San Francisco. At that time Treasure Island was there with bright lights and colored walls and soft music. It was beautiful. We had a wonderful day. When my wife and I left that night, we boarded the ferry and we went up to the top deck. We were country—we wanted to see the whole thing. As we watched, Treasure Island began to fade away into the fog, and the music died out. I said to my wife, "I have had one of the most pleasant days of my life. I enjoyed every bit of it. But if right now Treasure Island disappeared and went down under into the bay, I wouldn't shed a tear because I don't love anything that is over there." Then I added, "I hope I can always have that kind of an attitude toward the world."

Christian friend, do you really long for the coming of the Lord for the Rapture of the church? It is a wonderful thing to talk about, but I would like to ask you some questions: Will you weep when you leave this world because you are so wrapped up in it? Are you all wrapped up in a job or in a business, in a home or in some club, or in a worldly church? Would you be reluctant to go because everything will be changed? This is the way Simon Peter described the lost world:

"Which have forsaken the right way, and are gone astray, following the way of Balaam the son of Bosor, who loved the wages of unrighteousness; but was rebuked for his iniquity: the dumb ass speaking with man's voice forbad the madness of the prophet" (2 Pet. 2:15–16). This is a picture of the lost world. Do you as a child of God fit into this picture?

Before we knew Christ we walked "according to the prince of the power of the air," who is Satan. He was the energizer. We cannot serve both God and mammon. The one to whom we yield is our master. Even the Christian must choose whom he will serve. Some folk think that serving God means that you refrain from worldly dress and amusements and refuse associations with people who are liberal in their theology. That's not separation, yet that's what I hear today. It's absurd to talk like that when your own life is filled with bitterness and hatred and selfishness, which are the gross sins, by the way.

"Among whom also we all had our conversation in times past in the lusts of our flesh." Notice Paul now says "we." He includes himself; it is the first person, plural pronoun that he adopts. He puts himself right with this crowd, and you and I need to do this also. This verse could be amplified to read: "Among whom also we all had our conversation (our activities, our life-style) in times past in the desires of the flesh (that is, our old nature), doing the desires of the flesh and of the thoughts (our old nature and our mind), and we were by nature children of wrath even as others." Unfortunately, there are Christians who live for that old carnal nature. They live just like the man of the world is living today. Their life-style is prompted and motivated by a godless philosophy and is controlled by satanic principles.

I visited the home of a man who is supposed to be an outstanding Christian businessman. He showed me his lovely home and told me about his children. Then he told me about his business and about the honors that had been conferred upon him. He never once referred to his relationship with Jesus Christ. You see, there is something wrong with a life-style that includes everything in the world but leaves Christ out of it.

In this section of the second chapter of Ephesians Paul is giving a description of the past, present, and future of the church and of all believers. It is a common experience to see a sign up by a house that reads, "Your Future Told." Generally they have it figured out that soon you will come into a great fortune. The thing that always amuses me is that those places are usually in the poor section of town. They are not able to make a good living for themselves; yet they tell others that they will have a fortune coming to them. The Christian does not need to turn to such persons. God has already revealed to us our future as well as our past and present.

But God, who is rich in mercy, for his great love wherewith he loved us,

Even when we were dead in sins, hath quickened us together with Christ, (by grace ye are saved;)

And hath raised us up together, and made us sit together in heavenly places in Christ Jesus [Eph. 2:4-6].

This little conjunction *but* is so important. But God, being rich in mercy, on account of His great love with which He loved us made us alive together with Christ. God is *rich* in mercy. He had mercy on me. He has had mercy on you. This is such a radical change from the first three verses, which are as black and hopeless as anything can be. Man is a complete failure. He is incapable of saving himself. God comes on this scene of death with His mercy. He does not have too little, too late. He has a surplus, for He is an infinite God who is rich in infinite mercy. He has what man needs. He has what you need. The only requirement is that you believe Him.

A poor woman from the slums of London was invited to go with a group of people for a holiday at the ocean. She had never seen the ocean before, and when she saw it, she burst into tears. Those around her thought it was strange that she should cry when such a lovely holiday had been given her. They asked her, "Why in the world are you crying?" Pointing to the ocean she answered, "This is the only thing I have ever seen that there was enough of." My friend, God has *oceans* of mercy. There is enough of it. He saves us by His grace.

What does it mean to be saved by the grace of God? We were dead in trespasses and sins and completely incapable of saving ourselves. God comes on the scene and by grace He reaches down to us. Why does He do it? He does not find the reason in us; He finds it in Himself. When God came down to deliver Israel, it wasn't because they were good and beautiful and were serving Him. They were not. They were a stiff-necked people. And they were idolators—they worshiped a golden calf out there in the wilderness. But God says that He heard their cry. Why did that appeal to Him? Because He loved them. He loves you and He loves me. However, He doesn't save us by His love. He saves us by His grace.

For years I had a Bible class in San Diego County. During that period Christian groups of young folk had worked on the beaches down there and had led quite a few of those young people to Christ. Some of them belonged to what we called the hippie group, but I want to say that I found many of them to be genuine believers. I have come to the place that I do not judge a man by his dress any more than I would judge a book by its cover. They had listened to our radio program and to our tapes and had used our books—but I didn't know that at that time. When I went down there for my first class one year, sitting on the first two rows were a bunch of these young people. I want to tell you, some of them were dressed in a very unusual manner! They had long hair and all that was associated with that culture. Very frankly, they shocked me at first, but I found out that they had their Bibles and notebooks, and some *spiritual* life, which you don't always find in our churches today. These young people were actually showing real life.

One young fellow who had been attending came up to me. He had on a funny hat with "Love, love, love" written all over it. He had on a funny coat with "Love, love, love" written all over it. He had "Love, love" on his trousers and even on his shoes. I asked, "Why in the world do you have 'love' written all over you?" "Man," he said, "God is love." "Well," I said, "I agree with you. Nothing could be truer than that." Then he added, "God saves us by His love." I answered. "I don't agree with that. God doesn't save us by His love. Can you give me a verse that says He does?" He scratched his head and thought a while and then admitted he couldn't think of one. "Well," he said, "if God doesn't save us by love, then how does He save us?" I answered, "Very frankly, I'm glad you asked me that question because the Bible says, 'By grace are ye saved through faith; and that not of yourselves: it is the gift of God: not of works, lest any man should boast.' God saves us by His grace." Then the boy wanted to know the difference. This is how I explained it to him: "God does love you. Don't lose sight of that. God loves all of us. But God cannot, on the basis of His love, open the back door of heaven and slip us in under cover of darkness. He can't let down the bars of heaven at the front door and bring us in because of His love. God is also light. God is the moral ruler of this universe. God is righteousness. He is holy and He is good. That adds up to one thing: God cannot do things that are wrong—that is, wrong according to His own standard. So God couldn't save us by love. Love had God strapped—we could say it put Him in a bind. He could love without being able to save. I thought you would quote John 3:16 to me. Let's look at what that verse says: 'For God so loved the world, that he gave his only begotten Son, that whosoever believeth in him should not perish, but have everlasting life.' Does it say God so loved the world that He saved the world? No, that's exactly what it doesn't say. God so loved this world that He gave His only begotten Son. You see, God couldn't save the world by love because He goes on to say, 'that whosoever believeth in him should not perish.' You and I are going to perish. We're lost sinners, and God still loves us, but the love of God can't bring us into heaven. God had to provide a salvation, and He paid the penalty for our sins. Now a God of love can reach out His hands to a lost world and say, 'If you will believe in My Son, because He died for you—if you will come on that basis—I can save you.' God doesn't save us by His love. God saves us by His grace."

Frankly, it is more wonderful this way. When I was a boy, I would get out of favor with my parents because of something I did wrong. But I can never get out of the favor of God. I can lose my fellowship with Him, because sin breaks fellowship, but I can never get out of His favor. I can grieve the Spirit of God, but I can always come back to

Him. "If we confess our sins, he is faithful and just to forgive us our sins, and to cleanse us from all unrighteousness" (1 John 1:9). If we walk in darkness and say that we have fellowship with Him, we are lying. "But if we walk in the light, as he is in the light, we have fellowship one with another, and the blood of Jesus Christ his Son cleanseth us from all sin" (1 John 1:7). If I walk in the light of the Word of God and I see that I have come short, the blood of Jesus Christ, God's Son, just keeps on cleansing me from all sin. Why? God does it by His grace. He is rich in mercy and grace.

God has His arms outstretched to a lost world and He says, "You may come if you will come My way." Let me remind you that this is God's universe, and He is doing things His way. You may think you have a better way, but you don't have a universe to rule. He makes the rules in His universe and you're going to have to come His way. He loves you; you can't keep Him from loving you. Neither can you keep the sun from shining, but you can get out of the sunshine. Sin, being out of the will of God, turning your back on Him, all these will keep you from experiencing the love of God. If you will come to Him through Christ, He will save you and you will experience His love. God is rich in mercy.

God has lifted us out of a spiritual graveyard. Our present position is that He has "raised us up together, and made us sit together in heavenly places in Christ Jesus." What is our future?

That in the ages to come he might shew the exceeding riches of his grace in his kindness toward us through Christ Jesus [Eph. 2:7].

I translate it this way: "In order that He might show forth in the ages which are coming the exceeding (overflowing, intense) riches of His grace in kindness toward us in Christ." Someday I am going to be on exhibit. Angels will go by and say, "See that fellow McGee. He was lost and wasn't worth saving, but he's here in heaven today. It is only through the grace and kindness of God that he was saved and brought here." That is going to be for the praise of God throughout eternity. I am not going to get any credit at all, but I'm going to be there, and that's good enough for me. I'm going to join that angelic host in singing praises to God because He saved me. This is the most wonderful expectation that we have—as far as I know. It is through grace. It is the "amazing grace," as the hymn writer John Newton put it, "that saved a wretch like me."

For by grace are ye saved through faith; and that not of yourselves: it is the gift of God:

Not of works, lest any man should boast [Eph. 2:8–9].

These are the great verses that consummate this section on the believer's past, present, and future. We were dead in trespasses and sin, God saved us by His grace, raising us now to heavenly places in Christ Jesus, and we will someday be in heaven displaying the grace of God. None of this depends on our own works or merit, "for by grace ye have been saved." Notice I have changed it to the literal phrase "*the* grace." The article points out that it is something special. The great emphasis is upon the grace of God. It is favor bestowed on the unworthy and undeserving.

Now don't come along and say, "I hope to be saved." If you have put your trust in Christ, you can say, "I *am* saved." Someone may say, "Oh, I wouldn't dare make a statement like that because I don't know what the future holds." Friend, your salvation rests upon the *grace* of God—not upon your faithfulness. You can be confident of this very thing, ". . . that he which hath begun a good work in you will perform it until the day of Jesus Christ" (Phil. 1:6). If you are a child of God, you may wander from Him, but He will always make a way back for you because it is by His grace and that alone that you are saved. You have a finished salvation. On the basis of what Christ has done for you and on the fact that the Holy Spirit has inclined you toward Christ and you have believed the Word of God and have trusted Him, you can say, "I am saved." It's not an "I hope so" salvation or an "I'll try" salvation. It is a salvation that is by the grace of God, by means of faith, and it is not of yourself. It is a gift of God.

The grace of God has been defined theologically as "unmerited favor." I like to speak of it as "love in action." Dr. Lewis Sperry Chafer, the man who taught me theology, made this important statement about God's grace and God's love in his book, *The Ephesian Letter Doctrinally Considered.*

> A sharp distinction is properly drawn between the compassionate love of God for sinners, and His grace which is now offered to them in Jesus Christ. Divine love and divine grace are not one and the same. God might love sinners with an unutterable compassion and yet, because of the demands of outraged divine justice and holiness, be unable to rescue them from a righteous doom. However, as has been before stated, if love shall graciously provide for the sinner all that outraged justice and holiness could ever demand, the love of God would then be free to act without restraint in behalf of those for whom the perfect substitutionary sacrifice was made. This is Christ's achievement on the cross. On the other hand, divine grace in salvation is the unrestrained compassion of God acting toward the sinner on the basis of that freedom already secured through the righteous judgment against sin—secured by Christ in His sacrificial death. Divine love might desire to save, yet be unable righteously to do so; but divine grace is free to act since Christ has died. It is to be observed, then, that the eternal purpose of God is not the manifestation of His *love* alone, though His love and His mercy are, like His grace, mentioned in this context and expressed in Christ's death; but it is rather the manifestation of His grace.

Out of God's infinite treasure chest He lavishes His grace upon sinners without restraint or hindrance.

Now faith is the instrumental cause of salvation. It is the only element that the sinner brings to the great transaction of salvation. Yet it too is the gift of God. I know someone will say to me, "Since faith is the gift of God and God hasn't given it to me, then I guess I'm not to blame if I don't believe." The answer is this: God has made it very clear that faith comes by hearing and hearing by the Word of God. If you want to trust Christ, you will have to listen to the Word of God. God will give faith to all who give heed to the message of the gospel.

We find this taught in 2 Corinthians. Moses had a veil over his face, not because he was blinding everybody like a headlight, but so that the people could not view the glory that was fading away. It was the glory that belonged to the Mosaic system and that belonged to the Law. "But their minds were blinded: for until this day remaineth the same veil untaken away in the reading of the old testament; which veil is done away in Christ" (2 Cor. 3:14). There is no need for a veil today because He is the unveiled Christ; the gospel is freely declared. But we are told, "But even unto this day, when Moses is read, the veil is upon their heart. Nevertheless when it shall turn to the Lord, the veil shall be taken away" (2 Cor. 3:15–16). What is "it"? It is the heart. When the heart shall turn to the Lord, the veil shall be taken away. Anytime that you are ready to turn to Christ, you can turn to Christ.

Someone else objects, "Maybe I'm not given the gift of faith." That's not your problem. Your problem is that you don't want to give up your sins which the Bible condemns. Whenever you get sick of your sins, when you want to turn from yourself, from the things of the world, from religion, from everything the Bible condemns, and turn to Christ, then you will be given faith. You can trust Him.

I am weary of hearing folk say they don't believe because they have intellectual problems. Actually they have moral rather than intellectual problems if only they would face up to them. Sin is the real problem in the hearts of a great many folk today. Even many of the saints don't enjoy their salvation for that very reason. Psychologists at Duke University made a study and found that the second most frequent reason people are emotionally disturbed and mentally unstable is because they live in the past. They are preoccupied with past mistakes and failures, and they look to themselves instead of looking to Christ and trusting Him.

Faith is that instrument of salvation. Spurgeon says, "It is not thy joy in Christ that saves thee; it is Christ. It is not thy hope in Christ that saves thee; it is Christ. It is not even thy faith in Christ, though that be the instrument; it is Christ's blood and merit." That is where the power is, and that is where the salvation is.

Paul is not talking about *faith* when he says, "And that not of yourselves." He is talking about *salvation*. Salvation is a gift that eliminates boasting. It is all of God and not of us. It is God's *gift*.

For we are his workmanship, created in Christ Jesus unto good works, which God hath before ordained that we should walk in them [Eph. 2:10].

"We are his workmanship." The Greek word is *poiema* from which we get our word *poem*. The church is His poem and His new creation. Paul is not talking about the local church here, but rather about the body of believers from the day of Pentecost to the Rapture, the *real* believers (and most of them are members of local churches). That body of believers is His workmanship and His new creation in Christ Jesus.

For what are we created? For good works. When we get to the last part of this epistle, we will be told how we are to walk in a way that is creditable and acceptable to God. While we are seated in the heavenlies in Christ Jesus, we are to walk down here in a way that will bring glory to His name.

THE METHOD OF CONSTRUCTION

Now we come to the method of the construction of the church as a temple of God.

Wherefore remember, that ye being in time past Gentiles in the flesh, who are called Uncircumcision by that which is called the Circumcision in the flesh made by hands;

That at that time ye were without Christ, being aliens from the commonwealth of Israel, and strangers from the covenants of promise, having no hope, and without God in the world [Eph. 2:11–12].

The church in Ephesus was made up largely of Gentiles. There was just a small colony of Jews there. Gentiles are further identified as the "Uncircumcision." This label was put on them by the so-called "Circumcision," the Jews.

God made a real distinction between Jew and Gentile, beginning with Abraham and advancing to the advent of the Holy Spirit at Pentecost. Israel occupied a unique position among the nations. A Gentile could come in only as a proselyte. In time, this valid distinction caused friction because Israel became proud of her position. Israelites came to look down to Gentiles, and hatred crept into the hearts of both groups.

In these verses there is a description of the sad lot and hopeless plight of the Gentile. It is also an accurate picture of any lost man. This is what it means to be lost:

1. "Without Christ." That is the best definition of a lost man. It is the opposite of being in Christ.

2. "Aliens from the commonwealth of Israel" or, alienated from the citizenship of Israel. That is the accurate definition of a Gentile. The Gentile had no God-given religion as had Israel. They had no right to go back in the Old Testament and take the promises which God made to Israel and then appropriate them for themselves. We don't have that right either. God didn't make those promises to us.

3. "Strangers from the covenants of promise." God had made certain promises to the nation Israel. The covenants which God made with Israel are still valid, but no Gentile has any right to appropriate them. God has promised the children of Israel the land of Israel—all of it. They will get it someday, but it will be on God's terms, not their terms.

When I was in Israel, I didn't attempt to homestead or stake out a claim on the basis that God had promised it in the Old Testament. I understood that He was talking to Israel and not to me. The promise He has given to me is, ". . . I go to prepare a place for you, and if I go and prepare a place for you, I will come again, and receive you unto myself: that where I am, there ye may be also" (John 14:2–3).

4. "Having no hope." Look at the religions of the world. They have no hope. They cannot promise resurrection and are pretty hazy about

what happens after death. The cults offer no hope at all. They put up a hurdle that no honest human being could get over. Having no hope was the tragic plight of the Gentiles. To the lost man the present life is all-important, and if he misses out on the fun here, then he is doubly hopeless.

When Paul wrote this, my ancestors from one side of the family were walking through the forests of Germany, as heathen and pagan as they could be. The others were over in Scotland, and I am told their paganism and heathenism were even worse. That was our condition.

5. "And without God in the world." This does not mean that God has removed Himself from man, but rather that man has removed himself from God. A man is godless because of choice. He is in the darkness, wandering about with the rest of lost humanity. Frankly, if I were in the position of the lost man today, I would crawl up on a bar stool and try to drink and forget it all. What else would a person do? I would have no hope. The only hope I could have here in this world would be to squeeze this life like an orange and get all the juice out of it that I could. There would be nothing to look forward to over there. That is what it would be like to be without hope and without God.

This is a terrible, awful condition that Paul describes. But now notice that something has happened.

But now in Christ Jesus ye who sometimes were far off are made nigh by the blood of Christ [Eph. 2:13].

In the temple was the court of the Gentiles way off to the side. Gentiles were permitted to come, but they were away far off. But now—for the Gentiles who are in Christ—all has changed. They were without Christ; now they are in Christ. The distance and barriers which separated them from God have been removed. They have been made nigh, not by their efforts or merits, but by the blood of Christ.

For he is our peace, who hath made both one, and hath broken down the middle wall of partition between us;

Having abolished in his flesh the enmity, even the law of commandments contained in ordinances; for to make in himself of twain one new man, so making peace;

And that he might reconcile both unto God in one body by the cross, having slain the enmity thereby:

And came and preached peace to you which were afar off, and to them that were nigh [Eph. 2:14–17].

When you come to Jesus Christ, you are not only brought into a body, but you are also brought into a place where you stand before God on a par with anybody. I stand with you and you stand with me on equal footing. So today there should never be a point of separation for believers on any basis at all. We have been made one in Christ. If you are a believer in Christ—it makes no difference who you are—you and I are going to be together throughout eternity. It wouldn't be a bad idea for us to speak to each other every now and then down here, would it?

The contrast in the passage is really between the Jew and Gentile. The Lord Jesus Christ is the peace that has been made between them. The middle wall, the fence, or partition, the enmity between the two, has been broken down. He has made a new man. We have been put together in Christ, and He has made peace. It means that we now have peace with God, and we should also have peace with each other.

God's reconciliation is already complete. He is ready to receive you if you are ready to come. Therefore, the message that goes out is ". . . be ye reconciled to God" (2 Cor. 5:20). If you will be reconciled, you will be brought into a new body, a body of believers, and it doesn't make any difference whether you are Jew or Gentile. The color of your skin makes no difference. White, brown, red, black—all are one in Christ. We have been made one new man, and we should have peace.

The emphasis in this passage is upon the glorious person of Christ. He not only made peace by the Cross, but those who trust Him are placed in Him and become new men. God had made a difference originally by separating the Jew from the nations. The Jew eventually developed a spiritual pride, and this led to the ultimate hatred between Jew and Gentile. When a Jew and a Gentile are placed in Christ, there is peace. There is peace not only because of the new position, but also because something new has come into existence. Paul identifies this as a new man. That is why Paul wrote to the Corinthians, "Give none offence, neither to the Jews, nor to the Gentiles, nor to the church of God" (1 Cor. 10:32). That "church" is the new man.

It is not that the Gentile has been elevated to the status of the Jew. God has elevated both to a higher plane. Chrysostom has stated it this way: "He does not mean that He has elevated us to that high dignity of theirs, but He has raised both us and them to one still higher. . . . I will give you an illustration. Let us imagine that there are two statues, one of silver and the other of lead, and then that both shall be melted down, and the two shall come out gold. So thus He has made the two one." This is a marvelous illustration of how we have been brought together in Christ.

I do not believe in the universal brotherhood of man and the universal Fatherhood of God. To me that is a damnable heresy. I believe a true brotherhood is composed of those who are in Christ. A man may have skin as white as the driven snow, but if he is not a child of God, he is not my brother. A man may have skin as black as midnight, and if he is a child of God, he is my brother. We are something new. We are in Christ—a new man. This is the building, the temple, God is building today.

Rather than say the Gentile was elevated to the status of the Jew, one might say the Jew was brought down to the level of the Gentile because both Jew and Gentile are in the same state of sin. Actually we are all brothers as sinners, all sons of Adam. "What then? are we better than they? No, in no wise: for we have before proved both Jews and Gentiles, that they are all under sin" (Rom. 3:9). That is the state we were all in. The peace referred to is between the Jew and the Gentile. When the Jew and Gentile come to the Cross as sinners, they are made into a new creation. They become a new man, the body of Christ, the temple of the Holy Spirit.

The Old Testament temple which succeeded the Mosaic tabernacle was marked by partitions. There were three entrances into the three

departments: the outer court, the Holy Place, and the H.
Then there were sections partitioned off for priests, Israe.
and Gentiles. Christ, by His death, took out the veil, and He ̖
the Way (the outer court), the Truth (the Holy Place), and the Life ̖
Holy of Holies). Now we come through Christ directly into the pres
ence of God the Father. Those who come to Him are removed from
their little departments and are placed in Christ, the new Temple
where there are no departments. The Cross dissolves the fences, and
the gospel is preached to the Gentiles, those who were afar off, and to
the Jews, those who were near. What a picture we have here!

> **For through him we both have access by one Spirit unto
> the Father [Eph. 2:18].**

I wonder whether you have noticed that this little verse is a big verse?
It is like a little atom. It has in it the Trinity. "For through Him [Christ]
we both have access in one Spirit [the Holy Spirit] unto the Father [God
the Father]." Jew and Gentile are on the same footing as sinners at the
foot of the cross. In addition, through Christ they both have equal access to God, which is a glorious privilege for any human being. Paul
makes it clear in Romans 5 that justification by faith is a benefit available to all. We have access to God through Jesus Christ, and that is
wonderful.

Now I don't think this means we can brazenly rush into the presence of God, but it does give us the real privilege to have access to the
Father through the Lord Jesus Christ. Any one believer has as much
access to God as any other believer. People ask me why I didn't have a
select few pray for me when I had my bout with cancer. Why did I ask
everybody to pray? I did it because I believe in the priesthood of believers, that is, all believers have access to Him.

THE MEANING OF THE CONSTRUCTION

> **Now therefore ye are no more strangers and foreigners,
> but fellow-citizens with the saints, and of the household
> of God;**

> **And are built upon the foundation of the apostles and prophets, Jesus Christ himself being the chief corner stone [Eph. 2:19–20].**

Paul reminds the gentile believers that though they were strangers and alienated from God, their present position is infinitely bettered. They are no more strangers and sojourners (foreigners). They are now fellow citizens with the saints.

"Saints" is not a reference to Old Testament saints. Gentile believers are fellow citizens with the New Testament Jewish saints, the other members of the body of Christ. They belong to a household, not as servants, but as relatives, as members of the family of God. They are His dear children. "I write unto you, little children, because your sins are forgiven you for his name's sake" (1 John 2:12). We are little children. This is a new relationship, a relationship foreign to the Old Testament. Even David, the man after God's own heart, is called "my servant David" in 2 Samuel 7:8; and God's term for Moses was also "my servant" in Numbers 12:7.

Now this citizenship is not in Israel and the earthly Jerusalem, but it is in heaven. "For our conversation [citizenship] is in heaven; from whence also we look for the Saviour, the Lord Jesus Christ" (Phil. 3:20). We are now fellow citizens. We belong to heaven at the present time. The word *conversation* should rightly be changed to *citizenship* and is translated that way in the *American Standard Version*. Another has well translated it, "Our city home is in heaven."

We are "built upon the foundation of the apostles and prophets." This is important. It does not mean that the apostles and prophets were the foundation but that they personally laid the foundation. The early church built its doctrine upon that of the apostles. "And they continued stedfastly in the apostles' doctrine and fellowship, and in breaking of bread, and in prayers" (Acts 2:42).

Much has been written about the identity of the prophets in verse twenty. Are they Old Testament prophets or New Testament prophets? The fact that the prophets are in the same classification as apostles without the article *the* would seem to designate them as New Testament prophets. I think you will find this confirmed when we get into the third chapter.

"Jesus Christ himself being the chief corner stone" reveals that Christ is the Rock on which the church is built. Paul makes this very clear: "For other foundation can no man lay than that is laid, which is Jesus Christ" (1 Cor. 3:11). Peter states it like this: "Wherefore also it is contained in the scripture, Behold, I lay in Zion a chief corner stone, elect, precious: and he that believeth on him shall not be confounded. Unto you therefore which believe he is precious: but unto them which be disobedient, the stone which the builders disallowed, the same is made the head of the corner, and a stone of stumbling, and a rock of offence, even to them which stumble at the word, being disobedient: whereunto also they were appointed" (1 Pet. 2:6–8). The important thing to note here is that Peter says that the Lord Jesus is that chief cornerstone. Therefore Peter understood what the Lord meant when He said, "And I say also unto thee, That thou art Peter, and upon this rock I will build my church; and the gates of hell shall not prevail against it" (Matt. 16:18). Jesus is talking about Himself. He is the Rock on which the church is built. The apostles and prophets put down the foundation, and Christ is the chief cornerstone, the Rock.

In whom all the building fitly framed together groweth unto an holy temple in the Lord:

In whom ye also are builded together for an habitation of God through the Spirit [Eph. 2:21–22].

The analogy to the temple of the Old Testament is obvious; yet there is a contrast revealed in the analogy. There were several buildings in the temple at Jerusalem. However, I don't think Paul is referring to the different buildings. He means each individual believer is fitted into the total structure. Peter expressed it in the same way when he wrote that we are stones fitted in and built into a spiritual house (see 1 Pet. 2:5).

Paul speaks of the church as a temple which is currently under construction. That is quite interesting because in Paul's day Herod's temple was unfinished. It had been forty years in the building already in our Lord's day, and it was destroyed in A.D. 70. Even when it was destroyed, it had not yet been completely built. The church is under construction today, and it will be finished.

"Groweth unto an holy temple"—it is growing unto an holy temple in the Lord. This confirms the fact that it is still unfinished. The structure is also different. It is not one stone put on top of another in a cold way. This temple is growing. God is taking dead material, dead in trespasses and sins, and is giving it life. The living, born again, stones are growing into a living temple.

As Solomon's temple was built without the sound of hammer, so the Holy Spirit silently places each dead sinner into the living temple through regeneration and baptism. "For by one Spirit are we all baptized into one body, whether we be Jews or Gentiles, whether we be bond or free; and have been all made to drink into one Spirit" (1 Cor. 12:13).

It is called "an holy temple" or holy sanctuary. It is holy because the Holy Spirit indwells it. By the baptism of the Holy Spirit the saved sinner is placed "in the Lord." The Holy Spirit indwells each believer. "But ye are not in the flesh, but in the Spirit, if so be that the Spirit of God dwell in you. Now if any man have not the Spirit of Christ, he is none of his" (Rom. 8:9).

The church, the body of Christ, is "an habitation," a permanent temple, of God in the Spirit. When believers come together in a building to worship, the Holy Spirit is present. In that sense God is in that building. But when every believer has left the building, God has left it also. God is not in any church building anymore than He is in any barroom. Today God indwells believers, not buildings. We have previously stated that God has never dwelt in any building made with hands, and it is a pagan philosophy which places God in a human-made structure.

The purpose of the church as a temple is to reveal the presence and the glory of God on earth. When believers assemble together in a church, the impression should be made upon the world, even in this age, that God is in His holy temple. The world should feel that God can be found in a church service. My question is: Can He? Perhaps more people would be attracted to the church if they were sure that God was present.

CHAPTER 3

THEME: The church is a mystery; the explanation of
the mystery; the definition of the mystery; prayer for
power and knowledge

This is the final chapter in the doctrinal section of this epistle. We
have learned that the church is a body and the church is a temple.
Now we learn that the church is a mystery.

Let me give a preliminary word about what it means when we say
the church is a mystery. There has been gross misunderstanding concerning the church as a mystery. The word for *mystery* bears no re-
semblance to the modern connotation of "whodunit?" In this sense, a
mystery is something that had not previously been revealed but is currently made manifest. In this case it is the church which was not revealed in the Old Testament but is solely revealed in the New
Testament. Moffatt translates the word *mystery* as "divine secret," and
Weymouth uses the word "truth." I like the expression "divine secret." A divine secret was something that God had not revealed up to a
certain point. Now He is ready to reveal it. It has nothing to do with
mystery such as those written by Agatha Christie or Conan Doyle, as I
mentioned earlier when we discussed *mystery* in the first chapter.

There are two extreme viewpoints taken in our day concerning the
mystery of the church, and I must say that these viewpoints are a mystery to me. One extreme group ignores the clear-cut statement of Paul
that the church is *not* a revelation of the Old Testament. They treat the
church as a continuation of Israel. This is known as covenant theology. They appropriate all the promises that God made to Israel and
apply them to the church.

Years ago Dr. Harry Ironside showed me a Bible used by the group
holding the covenant theology viewpoint. In the books of the Old Testament prophets, they had headed some of the chapters: "Blessings for
the Church." Other chapters were headed: "Curses for Israel." It's quite
interesting that the church took the blessings but left the curses for

Israel! The truth is that both the blessings and the curses apply to Israel.

The other group places undue emphasis on Paul's statements: "he made known unto me the mystery," and "my knowledge in the mystery of Christ," and they treat the mystery as the peculiar revelation to Paul. This is known as hyperdispensationalism. As a result there has been the pernicious practice of shifting the beginning of the church to some date after Pentecost. On this sliding scale several dates have been suggested, and when one becomes untenable, another is adopted. This claim to superior knowledge has ministered to spiritual pride. May I say that the church was not revealed in the Old Testament. When it was revealed, the revelation was not confined to the apostle Paul. One professor I had in a denominational seminary tried to trace the church back to the Garden of Eden! But the church is not in the Old Testament. On the other hand, one must admit something happened on the Day of Pentecost. On that day the Holy Spirit began forming the body of believers. That will continue until He takes the church out of the world. We are sealed by the Holy Spirit of God until the day of redemption, the day we are taken out of the world and presented to Christ. I don't believe you can wash back and forth over the Day of Pentecost like the tide washing over the beach. Something *did* happen on that day—that was the birthday of the church.

THE EXPLANATION OF THE MYSTERY

For this cause I Paul, the prisoner of Jesus Christ for you Gentiles,

If ye have heard of the dispensation of the grace of God which is given me to you-ward [Eph. 3:1–2].

Let me give you my literal translation: "For this cause I Paul, the prisoner of (the) Christ Jesus on behalf of you Gentiles, if so be (upon the supposition) that ye heard of the economy (dispensation) of the grace of God which is given me to you."

Paul speaks of his present condition as a prisoner. He became a prisoner because he took the gospel to the Gentiles. Now the Gentiles are accorded new privileges, which he has enumerated in the preceding chapter. Those who were afar off, strangers, without hope, and without God, are now brought in through Christ. Because of all that, Paul is going to pray for them. But before he gets to his prayer, he digresses to speak of the mystery. Then he picks up his thread of thought again in verse 14. Notice the connection: "For this cause I Paul, the prisoner of Jesus Christ for you Gentiles. . . . bow my knees unto the Father of our Lord Jesus Christ." Everything between verses 1 and 14 is a parenthesis, a digression. Before he comes to his prayer, he is going to talk about the mystery.

"If so be" marks the beginning of the parenthesis. It is on the supposition that "ye have heard of the economy (or dispensation) of the grace of God which is given me to you." Paul is speaking of the divine plan and arrangement by which God had called and sent him to the Gentiles. As compared to the other apostles, Paul's ministry was different and special. "But contrariwise, when they saw that the gospel of the uncircumcision was committed unto me, as the gospel of the circumcision was unto Peter" (Gal. 2:7). The message was not different, but the ones to whom the message was to be given were different folk in a different category. Paul went to the Gentiles and told them, "You have been afar off, and now you can be brought in through Christ." Peter went to his own people (Israel) and said, ". . . there is none other name under heaven given among men, whereby we must be saved" (Acts 4:12). Paul said to the gentile, Philippian jailor, ". . . Believe on the Lord Jesus Christ, and thou shalt be saved, and thy house" (Acts 16:31). Both Peter and Paul had the same message, although it was to two different groups of people.

There is now a brand new thing taking place. It is a different economy or a different dispensation from what they had back in the Old Testament. When Paul had been a Pharisee and lived by the Law, he never went out to preach to the Gentiles—he was under a different economy. Now Paul is under a new economy, and he is a missionary to the Gentiles. This doesn't mean that God's method of salvation had changed. No man was saved by keeping the Law, but by bringing a bloody sacrifice when he saw that he had come short of the glory of God. That sacrifice pointed to Christ.

Now Paul is going to talk about this new economy.

How that by revelation he made known unto me the mystery; (as I wrote afore in a few words,

Whereby, when ye read, ye may understand my knowledge in the mystery of Christ) [Eph. 3:3–4].

"By revelation." The hyperdispensationalists hold that because Paul said the mystery had been made known to him, he was the only one who knew it. However, in verse 5 Paul makes it clear that all the apostles knew it. That "revelation" began with Paul's conversion when Christ informed him that when he persecuted the church he was actually persecuting Christ. The church is the body of Christ. Paul learned that God was doing something new. A church had come into existence on the Day of Pentecost.

I repeat that "the mystery," the divine secret, was something not revealed in the Old Testament and therefore unknown to man. Now it is revealed in the New Testament. The word is used twenty-seven times in the New Testament, and it refers to about eleven different mysteries. Paul seems to be making a contrast with the mystery religions of the Graeco-Roman world. In my book *Exploring Through Ephesians* I include a thesis on those mystery religions that I wrote when I was in seminary. There were many in that day. These were secret lodges in which sadistic rites were performed. The initiate was warned not to reveal the secrets of the mystery religion. To the Greek, a mystery was a secret imparted to the initiate. To them it meant something disclosed or revealed to a candidate for admission, not something hidden or impossible to understand. To the man on the street who was not a member, these secrets would be a mystery in our sense of the word. In contrast to this, Paul says, "Woe is me if I preach not the gospel." And we today are "stewards of the mysteries of God." We are to give out the message. The gospel is not something to be kept in a secret lodge; it is the good news that is to be shouted from the housetops.

Paul uses the word *mystery* earlier in this epistle. In Ephesians 1:9 he says, "Having made known unto us the mystery of his will." In Ephesians 2:14–15 he explains what the mystery is. The mystery is that Christ is risen and is the Head of a new body made up of Jews and Gentiles and of all tribes and peoples of the earth. This was not revealed in the Old Testament. Paul put it like this: "Now to him that is of power to stablish you according to my gospel, and the preaching of Jesus Christ, according to the revelation of the mystery, which was kept secret since the world began" (Rom. 16:25). Paul says it again in Colossians 1:26, "Even the mystery which hath been hid from ages and from generations, but now is made manifest to his saints."

I would say that those who insist that the church is back in the Old Testament are more or less usurping the place of the Lord. They are telling something the Lord Himself didn't tell. They act as if they know something God didn't know. Mystery means that it was not revealed in the Old Testament. And since He didn't reveal it, it isn't there.

THE DEFINITION OF THE MYSTERY

Which in other ages was not made known unto the sons of men, as it is now revealed unto his holy apostles and prophets by the Spirit;

That the Gentiles should be fellow-heirs, and of the same body and partakers of his promise in Christ by the gospel [Eph. 3:5–6].

Paul certainly makes it clear here that this was not revealed to him alone.

Now he clarifies what he means by the mystery. There is a sharp contrast between the sons of men in past generations and the apostles and prophets of the church. No one in the Old Testament had a glimmer of light relative to the church. It is now revealed to His Holy apostles. They are "holy" because they have been set aside for this office by God. The "prophets" are definitely New Testament prophets.

The "Spirit," the Holy Spirit, is the teacher of this mystery. This is what the Lord Jesus promised when He told His disciples of the coming of the Holy Spirit. "All things that the Father hath are mine: therefore said I, that he shall take of mine, and shall shew it unto you" (John 16:15).

What precisely is the mystery? It is *not* the fact that Gentiles would be saved. The Old Testament clearly taught that Gentiles would be saved. Let me cite several passages: "And in that day there shall be a root of Jesse, which shall stand for an ensign of the people; to it shall the Gentiles seek: and his rest shall be glorious" (Isa. 11:10). Another: "And the Gentiles shall come to thy light, and kings to the brightness of thy rising" (Isa. 60:3). Isaiah also wrote: "I the LORD have called thee in righteousness, and will hold thine hand, and will keep thee, and give thee for a covenant of the people, for a light of the Gentiles" (Isa. 42:6). Zechariah also mentions it: "And many nations shall be joined to the LORD in that day, and shall be my people: and I will dwell in the midst of thee, and thou shalt know that the LORD of hosts hath sent me unto thee" (Zech. 2:11). And Malachi: "For from the rising of the sun even unto the going down of the same my name shall be great among the Gentiles; and in every place incense shall be offered unto my name, and a pure offering: for my name shall be great among the heathen, saith the LORD of hosts" (Mal. 1:11).

If the mystery is not that the Gentiles would be saved, what is the mystery? Mark it carefully. The mystery was that the Gentiles and Israel were placed *on the same basis.* By faith in Christ they were both brought into a new body which is the church. Christ is the Head of that new body.

Therefore, now there is a threefold division in the human race:

All people were Gentiles from Adam to Abraham—2000 years (plus)

All people were either Jews or Gentiles from Abraham to Christ—2000 years

The threefold division is Jews, Gentiles, and the church from the Day of Pentecost to the Rapture—2000 years (plus)

Paul referred to this threefold division when he said, "Give none offence, neither to the Jews, nor to the Gentiles, nor to the church of God" (1 Cor. 10:32). Paul included the whole human family when he said that.

The church is not in the Old Testament *de facto*, although there are types of it in the Old Testament. Christ said, ". . . upon this rock I *will* build my church . . ." (Matt. 16:18, italics mine), and when He spoke that, it was still future. The church began on the Day of Pentecost, after Christ had returned to heaven. To say that the church began beyond the Day of Pentecost makes the church a pair of Siamese twins— a Jewish church and a Gentile church coexisting. It is true that the church was all Jewish when it began, but there was a period of transition when Gentiles were brought into it. The church is one body, made up of both Jew and Gentile, and Christ is the Head of that body.

Whereof I was made a minister, according to the gift of the grace of God given unto me by the effectual working of his power [Eph. 3:7].

Paul assumed no place of superiority in the knowledge of the mystery by virtue of the fact that he was the Apostle to the Gentiles. He takes only the title of *diakonos* which is translated "minister" and means a worker or helper or deacon.

It was the gift of God's grace which had transformed him from Saul, the proud Pharisee who persecuted the church, to Paul, the apostle who was now a prisoner for Jesus Christ. He had been taken out of one group and put into another. He is now a member of the body of Christ. All that had been accomplished was through the working of the power of the Holy Spirit. Paul had both the gift and the power of an apostle.

Unto me, who am less than the least of all saints, is this grace given, that I should preach among the Gentiles the unsearchable riches of Christ;

And to make all men see what is the fellowship of the mystery, which from the beginning of the world hath been hid in God, who created all things by Jesus Christ [Eph. 3:8–9].

We are living today in the economy, or the dispensation, or the mystery of the church (the gospel of grace), which from the ages past has been hid in God who created all things. My friend, there are a lot of things God has not told us yet, which is one of the reasons I am anticipating heaven. If you think I don't know very much now, you are right. When I get to heaven, I am really going to start learning things. Really, God hasn't told us very much. It's amazing to think how little He has told us. For example, He never told anybody about that little atom. Nor did He tell anybody that there were diamonds deep in the earth. He has kept a lot of things to Himself. He allows man to make discoveries, but there are some things man can never find out except by revelation. The church was a mystery in that sense.

In verse 8 Paul calls himself "less than the least of all saints"—it is a comparative superlative. Paul always took the place of humility as an apostle. "For I am the least of the apostles, that am not meet to be called an apostle, because I persecuted the church of God" (1 Cor. 15:9). "And I thank Christ Jesus our Lord, who hath enabled me, for that he counted me faithful, putting me into the ministry; who was before a blasphemer, and a persecutor, and injurious: but I obtained mercy, because I did it ignorantly in unbelief" (1 Tim. 1:12–13).

A mighty revolution took place in the life of Paul. He was chosen to preach among the Gentiles the unsearchable riches of Christ. How wonderful!

"And to make all men see"—the mystery is not to be argued or debated but is to be preached. And Paul was to make all men see the economy (the dispensation) of the mystery.

To the intent that now unto the principalities and powers in heavenly places might be known by the church the manifold wisdom of God,

According to the eternal purpose which he purposed in Christ Jesus our Lord [Eph. 3:10–11].

Another purpose of the mystery is revealed here. God's created intelligences are learning something of the wisdom of God through the church. They not only see the love of God displayed and lavished upon us, but the wisdom of God is revealed to His angels.

In whom we have boldness and access with confidence by the faith of him [Eph. 3:12].

We, the Gentiles, and Paul, the persecutor, have freedom of speech before God and an access or introduction to Him. This is all made possible in Christ.

Wherefore I desire that ye faint not at my tribulations for you, which is your glory [Eph. 3:13].

He says, "I entreat you that you not lose heart in my troubles for you, which is your glory." Because of the great goals of the mystery which Paul has enumerated, he is willing to suffer imprisonment as the Apostle to the Gentiles. He didn't want the Ephesians to be discouraged, because the imprisonment of Paul was working for his good and their glory. "Who now rejoice in my sufferings for you, and fill up that which is behind of the afflictions of Christ in my flesh for his body's sake, which is the church" (Col. 1:24).

PRAYER FOR POWER AND KNOWLEDGE

For this cause I bow my knees unto the Father of our Lord Jesus Christ [Eph. 3:14].

What was the cause? It was because of his deep interest in these Ephesians. He wanted them to enter into the great truth of this dispensation, this new economy in which we live, and to experience all the riches of His grace in Christ Jesus. That was the background. That is why he inserted the parenthesis between verses 1 and 14.

We have already called attention to the fact that Paul was a man of prayer. This is the second great prayer of Paul in this epistle. As he viewed the church as the poem of God, the temple of the Holy Spirit, the mystery of the ages, he went to God in prayer that these great truths might become realities in the lives of believers.

In this verse we have another characteristic of the prayers of Paul. It reveals his posture in prayer. I do not want to be splitting hairs, but here it is: "I bow my knees unto the Father of our Lord Jesus Christ." I don't insist that we all get down on our knees in our public prayer meetings today. However, I rather wish that we did.

During my first pastorate in Nashville, Tennessee, I conducted a meeting in Stone's River Church near Murfreesboro, Tennessee. It was one of the best meetings I have ever had. It was a little country church, and when I began, I said, "Let's bow our heads in prayer." I shut my eyes and heard a rumbling. It sounded as if everyone was walking out; so I ventured a look. I didn't see a soul and thought they had really walked out on me. Since I was praying to the Lord, I just continued to pray. When I said, "Amen," I opened my eyes and these people came up out of the ground! They had all been down on their knees. We had a wonderful meeting. Now don't misunderstand me—I'm not saying we had a great meeting just because they were down on their knees, but I do want to say that I think it helped a great deal.

In the formality and ritual of our new churches with plush seats and carpeted floors we are missing something in our relationship to the Lord. My feeling is that there ought to be more easy familiarity with each other in our churches but more worship and reverence for God, especially at the time of prayer.

As creatures we ought to assume our proper place before our Creator and go down on all fours before Him. Paul prayed that way and I have always felt that was the proper posture. I must confess that since I have arthritis I don't do it like I used to when I would get down right on my face in my study and pray there. It is amazing how such a posture helps a person to pray. I think it is something that is good for man. I don't insist on this; I merely call your attention to it. This is the way Paul did it, and I think he is a very good example for us today. Aren't we told that our Lord went into the Garden of Gethsemane and fell on His face? I think it would be proper for us if we would get down on our faces before God.

There is another point which I think is rather important to note. We have here that Paul prayed to God the Father in the name of the Lord Jesus Christ. You will also notice that back in chapter 1, verse 17, he prayed to the "God of our Lord Jesus Christ." We find that this was his formula, and I think it is a rather tight formula to address all prayers to God the Father in the name of our Lord Jesus Christ. Someone may say, "Aren't you splitting hairs?" Listen to the Lord Jesus: "And in that day ye shall ask me nothing. Verily, verily, I say unto you, Whatsoever ye shall ask the *Father* in *my* name, he will give it you" (John 16:23, italics mine).

The disciples had been with our Lord for three years. I think they were like a group of children in many ways. I think it was, "Gimme, gimme" a great deal of the time. Then our Lord told them that He would be leaving them. After that they would not ask Jesus for anything. They were to direct their requests to the Father in the name of Jesus. What does Jesus mean by that? He means simply that if you and I were to pray to the Lord Jesus directly, we would rob ourselves of an intercessor. Jesus Christ is our great Intercessor. To pray in Jesus' name means we go to God the Father with a prayer that the Lord Jesus Himself can lift to the Father for you and me.

We need to be very careful in our prayer life. Now that I am retired, I notice things I never noticed before. I was in a service not long ago in which they called on a visiting brother to pray for the meetings at this conference. The conference had gotten off to a marvelous start. The music had been excellent, the pastor had presided well, then they called on this brother to pray. He prayed for a great many things, and I counted three times that he prayed for me. When he prayed for me the second time, my reaction was, *Well, you don't need to tell the Lord that again!* Then when he said it the third time, I thought, *He will turn the Lord off—He'll get tired of hearing that repetitious prayer.* Perhaps after this brother had looked me over he decided I really needed praying for three times! Nevertheless, it was vain repetition as the heathen use. The Lord heard him the first time. We need to be very careful in our prayer life.

Have you noticed that Paul's prayers are brief? Both prayers here in Ephesians and his prayer in Philippians are brief. In fact, all the prayers of Scripture are quite brief. The Lord Jesus said that we are not to use vain repetition as the heathen do—they think they will be heard for their much speaking. Moses' great prayer for Israel is recorded in only three verses. Elijah, on top of Mount Carmel as he stood alone for God against the prophets of Baal, prayed a great prayer which is only one verse long. Nehemiah's great prayer is recorded in only seven verses. The prayer of our Lord in John 17 takes only three minutes to read. But the briefest prayer is that of Simon Peter, ". . . Lord, save me" (Matt. 14:30). He cried out this prayer when he was beginning to sink beneath the waves of the Sea of Galilee. Some people think that was not a prayer because it was so short. My friend, that was a prayer, and it was answered immediately. If Simon Peter had prayed like some of us preachers pray on Sunday morning, "Lord, Thou who art the omnipotent, the omniscient, the omnipresent One. . . ." he would have been twenty feet under water before he got to his request. I tell you, he got down to business. Prayer should be brief and to the point.

Of whom the whole family in heaven and earth is named [Eph. 3:15].

God has a wonderful family. A great many folk think that it is only me and mine—we four and no more. But it's a little wider than that. Some folk feel that their little clique in the church is the only group the Lord is listening to. Some people think their local church constitutes the saints. Then there are others who think their denomination is the whole family of God. Then there are some who think it is just the church—that is, those saved from the Day of Pentecost to the Rapture. My friend, God saved people long before the church came into existence, and He is going to be saving people after the church leaves. Also God has other members of His family. The angels belong to His family. He has created intelligences which the apostle John saw and said cannot be numbered. All of those are the family of God.

That he would grant you, according to the riches of his glory, to be strengthened with might by his Spirit in the inner man;

That Christ may dwell in your hearts by faith; that ye, being rooted and grounded in love,

May be able to comprehend with all saints what is the breadth, and length, and depth, and height;

And to know the love of Christ, which passeth knowledge, that ye might be filled with all the fulness of God [Eph. 3:16–19].

Notice again that he prays *according to* the riches of His glory, not *out of* the riches of His glory. If He would take it out of His riches, He would be like Mr. Rockefeller who used to give his caddy a dime.

There are four definite petitions here which Paul makes on behalf of the Ephesian believers.

1. The petition is that the believers might "be strengthened with might [power] by his Spirit in the inner man." The spiritual nature of the believer needs prayer as well as does the physical. How often the spiritual is neglected while all the attention is given to the physical side. Paul prays for the inner man because he realizes that the outward man is passing away. Power is needed to live the Christian life, to grow in grace, and to develop into full maturity—which is the work of the Holy Spirit.

We tend to pray a great deal for the outward man. It is a marvelous way to pray, praying for the physical needs of folk. Paul did, and he prayed for himself. Three times he asked God to remove the thorn in his flesh. It is wonderful to know that God does hear and does answer prayer, but we need to remember that the spiritual nature of the believer needs prayer as well as the physical. Only the Holy Spirit can supply power, living, and growth for the full maturity of the believer.

2. In the second petition Paul prays that "Christ may dwell in your hearts by faith." This is to think the Lord's thoughts after Him. "Ye in me and I in you." Paul could exclaim, ". . . Christ liveth in me . . ." (Gal. 2:20). *In Christ* is the high word of this epistle. The

wonderful counterpart of it is that Christ is in us. In Christ—that is our position. Christ in us—that is our possession. That is the practical side of it. "Examine yourselves, whether ye be in the faith; prove your own selves. Know ye not your own selves, how that Jesus Christ is in you, except ye be reprobates?" (2 Cor. 13:5).

Christ has not come as a temporary visitor. He has come as a permanent tenant by means of the Spirit to live in our lives. "I am the vine, ye are the branches: he that abideth in me, and I in him, the same bringeth forth much fruit: for without me ye can do nothing" (John 15:5).

3. The third petition is a request that the believers may know the dimensions of the knowledge-surpassing love of Christ. He prays that they may be "rooted and grounded in love." "Rooted" refers to botany, to life. "Grounded" refers to architecture, to stability. This is for all the saints.

Paul wants them to "know the love of Christ, which passeth knowledge." The vast expanse of the love of Christ is the love of God Himself. From this launching pad we can begin to measure that which is immeasurable and to know that which passes knowledge. This is one of the many paradoxes of the believer's life.

The *breadth*. The arms of Christ reach around the world. "I am the door: by me if any man enter in, he shall be saved . . ." (John 10:9). ". . . him that cometh to me I will in no wise cast out" (John 6:37).

The *length*. The length of it begins with the Lamb slain before the foundation of the world and proceeds unto the endless ages of eternity.

The *depth*. The depth goes all the way to Christ's death on the cross. "And being found in fashion as a man, he humbled himself, and became obedient unto death, even the death of the cross" (Phil. 2:8).

The *height*. The height reaches to the throne of God. "Who, being in the form of God, thought it not robbery to be equal with God" (Phil. 2:6).

Only the Holy Spirit can lead a believer into this vast experience of the love of Christ. Since it is infinite, it is beyond human comprehension.

4. The fourth petition is a final outburst of an all-consuming fervor that believers "might be filled up to all the fulness of God." Christ was thus filled. In proportion to our comprehension of the love of Christ, we shall be filled with all the fullness of God.

Now unto him that is able to do exceeding abundantly above all that we ask or think, according to the power that worketh in us,

Unto him be glory in the church by Christ Jesus throughout all ages, world without end. Amen [Eph. 3:20–21].

This is both a doxology and a benediction which concludes the prayer of Paul. It also concludes the first main division of this epistle. This is a mighty outburst of spiritual praise, which any comment would only tarnish. We are not able to so much as touch the hem of the garment of the spiritual gifts that God is prepared to give to His own. How wonderful this is! He wants to give to us super-abundantly. How good He is, and how small we are. We cannot even contain all of His blessings.

CHAPTER 4

THEME: *The church is a new man; the exhibition of the new man; the inhibition of the new man; the prohibition of the new man*

We have now come to a new section of the Epistle to the Ephesians. The subjects of these last three chapters are the *conduct of the church* and the *vocation of the believer.* We have learned of the heavenly calling of the believer, and now we come to the believer's manner of life, his earthly walk. This is not a worldly walk, but it is an earthly walk. The true believers, which collectively we call the *church,* are seated in the heavenlies in Christ. Christ is the Head of the body and He is seated at God's right hand. But the church is to live down here on this earth.

In chapters 1—3 we have considered the *calling, construction,* and the *constitution* of the church. In this last section of the epistle we shall consider the *conduct* of the church, the *confession* of the church, and the *conflict* of the church. The church is a new man; in the future the church will be a bride; and the church is also a good soldier of Jesus Christ.

In the first three chapters we have been on the mountain peak of the Transfiguration, probably the highest spiritual point in the New Testament. That is the reason we spent so much time in those chapters. In this last division we descend to the plane of living where we confront a demon-possessed world and a skeptical mob. It is right down where the rubber meets the road. Are we able to translate the truths of the mountaintop into shoe leather? Are we able to stand and walk through the world in a way that is pleasing to God? Our Lord said that we are *in* the world but not *of* the world.

It has been stated that Ephesians occupies the same position theologically as the Book of Joshua does in the Old Testament. Now we come to the position where this truth is manifest. Joshua entered the

Land of Promise on the basis of the promise made to Abraham, Isaac, Jacob, and Moses. It was his by right of promise, and he led the children of Israel over the Jordan into the land. Passing over Jordan is symbolic of the death, burial, and resurrection of Christ. We as believers have been brought into the Promised Land. That is where you and I live—at least we *should* be living in resurrection territory today.

Joshua had to appropriate the land by taking possession of it for the enjoyment of it and for blessing in the land. *Possession* is the great word in the Book of Joshua. Although enemies and other obstacles stood in his way, Joshua had to overcome and occupy.

Position was a key word in the first half of Ephesians—God has blessed us "with all spiritual blessings" (Eph. 1:3). God has given them over to us, but are we walking down here in *possession* of them? The children of Israel had been promised their land, but it remained a "never-never" land to them until they entered it. "Every place that the sole of your foot shall tread upon, that have I given unto you, as I said unto Moses" (Josh. 1:3). God says, "Joshua, all of it is yours, but you will enjoy only that which you lay hold of."

Now the believer is privileged to move in and occupy "all spiritual blessings in the heavenlies." However, the unsearchable riches in Christ must be searched out with the spiritual Geiger counter, which is the Word of God. Up until now the epistle has been glorious declarations, but now there will be commands. Those who have been called to such an exalted place are now commanded to a way of life which is commensurate with the calling.

Some people dwell on the first part of the epistle and become rather super-duper saints, very spiritual. I remember a family like this when I first came to Southern California. They attended the church which I pastored but were not members. They were lovely, active people. I asked them one day why they didn't join the church. They looked up to the ceiling and said, "We're members of the *invisible* church," and fluttered their eyelids. I have learned that a lot of these folk who are members of the "invisible" church are *really* invisible— invisible on Sunday night and invisible on Wednesday night. In fact, they are invisible when you need help from them. Now, my friend, let's be practical about this: the invisible church is to make itself visible down here in a local assembly.

We have come to the practical side of Ephesians, the earthly conduct of the church; and in this chapter the church is portrayed as a new man. The new man is to exhibit himself down here. The members of the invisible church are to make themselves visible. They are to be extroverts, if you please, and they are to get out the Word of God.

What follows here is restricted to those who are in Christ. The Spirit of God is talking to saved people. If you are not a Christian, God is not asking you to do the commands in this epistle. First you must become a child of His through faith in Christ; you must become a member of His body. What follows in this epistle is for those who have been redeemed and have heard the Word of truth. Dead men cannot walk no matter how insistently they are urged to walk. The dead man must first be made alive. Paul has told us that we were dead in trespasses and sins. That is the condition of all who are lost. The top sergeant doesn't go out to the cemetery and yell, "Attention! Forward march!" If he did, there certainly wouldn't be any marching. Nobody would move. They must first have life. It is interesting that the religions are saying to a dying world, "Do something and you will be somebody." God says just the opposite: "Be somebody and then you can do something." If you are not a Christian, you just stay on the sidelines and listen. You will learn what God would ask of you if you are going to become a believer; and when you look around you, you will know whether or not the saints are living as God wants them to live.

THE EXHIBITION OF THE NEW MAN

I therefore, the prisoner of the Lord, beseech you that ye walk worthy of the vocation wherewith ye are called [Eph. 4:1].

"Therefore" is a connective, a transitional word. It is in view of all that God has done for the believer, which we have seen in the first three chapters of this epistle.

Paul is a "prisoner of the Lord." He is a prisoner because of his position in Christ. Isn't it interesting that Paul can be seated in the heavenlies in Christ and can also be seated in a prison because he was a witness for Christ to the Gentiles?

I "beseech [or beg] you that ye walk worthy of the vocation wherewith ye are called." This word for beseech or beg is the same word that we find in Romans 12:1. It is not the command of Sinai with fire and thunder; it is the gentle wooing of love: "I beseech you therefore, brethren, by the mercies of God . . ." (Rom. 12:1).

We are to "walk worthy" of our calling. It is a call to walk on a plane commensurate with the position we have in Christ. "Only let your conversation [that is, your manner of life or your life-style] be as it becometh the gospel of Christ: that whether I come and see you, or else be absent, I may hear of your affairs, that ye stand fast in one spirit, with one mind striving together for the faith of the gospel" (Phil. 1:27). Again Paul writes, "That ye might walk worthy of the Lord unto all pleasing, being fruitful in every good work, and increasing in the knowledge of God" (Col. 1:10). Paul points to his own life as an example of the Christian's walk: "Ye are witnesses, and God also, how holily and justly and unblameably we behaved ourselves among you that believe" (1 Thess. 2:10).

Paul begs us to walk worthy of the gospel. People may not be telling you this, but they are evaluating whether you are a real child of God through faith in Christ. The only way they can tell is by your walk. It's not so much *how* you walk as it is *where* you walk. "But if we walk in the light, as he is in the light, we have fellowship one with another, and the blood of Jesus Christ his Son cleanseth us from all sin" (1 John 1:7). Walking in "the light" is in the light of the Word of God. How much time do you really spend in the Word of God? Your children know how much time you spend in the Bible. Also your neighbors know, and the people in the church know. If we wish to walk in fellowship with God, we must walk in the light of the Word of God.

We have previously told the incident of a man handing out tracts, a ministry, by the way, that takes much prayer and intelligence. A black man who could neither read nor write was handed a tract. He asked,

"What is this?" When he was told it was a tract, he said, "Well I can't read it; so I'll watch your tracks." That was the greatest short sermon this Christian could ever have had preached to him. Someone was watching his tracks.

Paul does his beseeching on the basis of their calling. He has just explained to the Ephesians that they live in the economy of the grace of God. They live under that dispensation.

With all lowliness and meekness, with longsuffering, forbearing one another in love;

Endeavoring to keep the unity of the Spirit in the bond of peace [Eph. 4:2–3].

"Lowliness" means a mind brought low. Paul practiced what he preached. Lowliness means the opposite of pride. I wish our seminaries today would stop trying to make intellectual preachers and teach the young men to walk in lowliness of mind.

Years ago I heard the story of a very fashionable church in Edinburgh that wanted a pulpit-supply; so the seminary sent out to them a very fine young man who was brilliant in the classroom at the school. He had never had any experience, and he was filled with pride at ministering in this great church. When he got up before that group of people, he was struck with stage fright. He forgot everything he ever knew. He had memorized his sermon, but he forgot it. He stumbled through it and left the pulpit in humiliation, because he knew how miserably he had failed. A dear little Scottish lady went up to him and said, "Young man, I was watching you this morning, and I'd like to say to you that if you had gone up into that pulpit like you came down out of that pulpit, then you would have come down out of that pulpit like you went up into that pulpit." He had gone up with pride, but he had come down with lowliness and meekness.

Lowliness is the flagship of all Christian virtues. "Let nothing be done through strife or vainglory; but in lowliness of mind let each esteem other better than themselves" (Phil. 2:3). Lowliness characterized our Lord. He said, "Take my yoke upon you, and learn of me; for I am meek and lowly in heart . . ." (Matt. 11:29). There are too many Christians today who have a pride of race, a pride of place, a pride of face, and even a pride of grace—they are even proud that they have been saved by grace! Oh, how we need to walk in lowliness of mind!

The story is told of a group of people who went in to see Beethoven's home in Germany. After the tour guide had showed them Beethoven's piano and had finished his lecture, he asked if any of them would like to come up and sit at the piano for a moment and play a chord or two. There was a sudden rush to the piano by all the people except a gray-haired gentleman with long, flowing hair. The guide finally asked him, "Wouldn't you like to sit down at the piano and play a few notes?" He answered, "No, I don't feel worthy." That man was Paderewski, the only man who was really worthy to play the piano of Beethoven.

How often the saints rush in and do things when they have no gift for doing them. We say we have difficulty in finding folk who will do the work of the church, but there is another extreme—folk who attempt to do things for which they have no gift. We need to walk in lowliness of mind.

"With all lowliness and meekness." Meekness means mildness but it does not mean weakness. To be meek does not mean to be a Mr. Milquetoast. There are two men in Scripture who are noted for being meek. In the Old Testament it was Moses, and in the New Testament it was the Lord Jesus. When you see Moses come down from the mount and break the Ten Commandments written on the stone tablets and when you hear what he said to his brother Aaron and to the children of Israel, would you call that meekness? God called it that. When the Lord Jesus went in and drove the money changers out of the temple, was that meekness? It certainly was. The world has a definition of meekness and that makes it synonymous with weakness. The Bible calls meekness a willingness to stand and do the will of God regardless of the cost. Meekness is bowing yourself to the will of God.

"With longsuffering." Longsuffering means a long temper. This is a fruit of the Spirit (see Gal. 5:22). In other words, we should not have a short fuse. That is longsuffering.

"Forbearing one another in love" means to hold one's self back in the spirit of love. "Forbearing one another, and forgiving one another, if any man have a quarrel against any: even as Christ forgave you, so also do ye" (Col. 3:13).

"Endeavoring to keep the unity of the Spirit." The Lord Jesus prayed that we might be one: "That they all may be one; as thou, Father, art in me, and I in thee, that they also may be one in us: that the world may believe that thou hast sent me" (John 17:21). The Spirit of God has baptized us into one body. "For by one Spirit are we all baptized into one body, whether we be Jews or Gentiles, whether we be bond or free; and have been all made to drink into one Spirit" (1 Cor. 12:13). Now believers are to keep the unity which the Holy Spirit has made. We cannot *make* that unity. We cannot join into an ecumenical movement to force a kind of unity. Only the Holy Spirit makes the unity, but we are to maintain it. All true believers in Christ Jesus belong to one body, and we should realize that we are one in Christ.

Now he goes on to list seven of those unities:

There is one body, and one Spirit, even as ye are called in one hope of your calling;

One Lord, one faith, one baptism,

One God and Father of all, who is above all, and through all, and in you all [Eph. 4:4–6].

1. "One body" refers to the total number of believers from Pentecost to the Rapture. This one body is also called the invisible church, but this is not wholly accurate. All true believers should also be visible.

2. "One Spirit" refers to the Holy Spirit who baptizes each believer into the body of Christ. The work of the Holy Spirit is to unify believers in Christ. This is the unity that the believer is instructed to keep.

3. "One hope of your calling" refers to the goal set before all believers. They will be taken out of this world into the presence of Christ. This is the blessed hope (see Titus 2:13).

4. "One Lord" refers to the Lord Jesus Christ. His lordship over believers brings into existence the unity of the church.

5. "One faith" refers to the body of truth called the apostles' doctrine (see Acts 2:42). When this is denied, there are divisions. There must be substance to form an adhesion of believers. This substance is correct doctrine.

6. "One baptism" has reference to the baptism of the Holy Spirit, which is real baptism. Ritual baptism is by water. Water baptism is a symbol of the real baptism of the Holy Spirit by which believers are actually made one.

7. "One God and Father of all" refers to God's fatherhood of believers. Since there is only one Father, He is not the Father of unbelievers. Sonship can come only through Christ. The unity of believers produces a sharp distinction between believers and unbelievers. He is Father of all who are His by regeneration.

Paul has been talking about the church, the body of Christ, joined to Him who is in heaven at the right hand of the Father. The church is a new man. It is a mystery. This is all true because it is in Christ. Now some people can be so involved in these truths who are—as the saying goes—so heavenly-minded that they are no earthly good. Paul is trying to show that we still walk down here in a very evil, very sinful world.

In his discussion of this walk of the believer, Paul speaks first to the individual. The individual is to walk in lowliness and meekness. Then he widens out to the entire church, which is one body and one spirit. Finally, he brings this passage to a great, tremendous crescendo, which pictures the eminence and transcendence of God.

God is "above all, and through all, and in you all." This means that God is transcendent. He is above His creation. He is not dependent upon His creation. He doesn't depend upon oxygen to breathe. He doesn't have to bring up some supplies from the rear or go Saturday shopping in order to have food for the weekend. He is transcendent. He is not only transcendent, He is also eminent. He is not only above all, but He is through all and in you all. That means He is in this universe in which you and I live. He is motivating it and He is moving it according to His plan and purpose. That is what adds meaning to life. That is what makes life worthwhile.

Life gets a little humdrum now and then, doesn't it? There is a monotony to it. Although I love taping broadcasts for my radio program, sometimes when I'm in my study every day for a couple of weeks, it gets monotonous, and I get weary. But then I come to this great thought: all of this is in the plan and purpose of God. Then I feel like singing the doxology or the Hallelujah Chorus, and when I do, everybody moves out of earshot. But I can sing unto the Lord with a song that comes from my heart. The Bible says, ". . . making melody in your heart to the Lord" (Eph. 5:19), and that is where mine certainly comes from—not from my mouth, but from my heart.

This chapter reminds me of a great symphony orchestra. When I first went to Nashville as pastor, some friends asked me to go to the symphony with them. They thought they were doing me a favor, but there are other things I would rather do than go to a symphony concert. Although I'm not musically educated, and I don't understand music at all, I got a message at that concert. We had arrived early and I noticed all the instruments. It looked like over a hundred men came out from all the different wings and each went to his own instrument. My friends told me that they were "tuning up." Each one played his own little tune and, I give you my word, there was no melody in it. It was terrible! They quit after a few moments, for which I was thankful. Then they disappeared into the wings. Soon they all appeared again. This time they were in full dress with white shirts and bow ties. Each man came to his instrument, but no man dared play it. Then the spotlight went to the side of the stage and caught the conductor as he walked out. He bowed several times and there was thunderous applause. Then he picked up a little stick and turned his back to the audience. When he lifted that baton, you could have heard a pin drop in that auditorium, then when he lowered it—oh, what music came out of that great orchestra! I had never heard anything that was more thrilling. It made goose pimples come over me and made my hair stand on end.

After that first tremendous number, I got a little bored; I began comparing it with life on this earth. Out in the world every person is playing his own little tune. Everyone is trying to be heard above the clamor of voices or carrying his own little placard of protest. Everyone seems to be out of tune, out of harmony, with everyone else. It doesn't look very hopeful in the world today, and we look to the future with pessimism. Like Simon Peter walking on the lake, we see huge threatening waves. But one of these days there is going to step out from the wings of this universe, from God's right hand, the Conductor. He is called the King of Kings and the Lord of Lords. He will lift that baton, that scepter, with nail-pierced hands. When He does that, the whole world will be in tune. He is eminent and He is transcendent. He is "above all, through all, and in you all." So don't give up—the Conductor is coming. He will get us all in tune.

The church is to walk as a new man in this world. There is to be an exhibition. The church is to be an extrovert, to witness, to manifest life.

THE INHIBITION OF THE NEW MAN

Now we find that the church also has inhibitions and these are also important.

A little child doesn't have inhibitions. I think of a time when I visited some people who were church members. They put on quite a performance of how pious and how religious they were. When we sat down at the table, they called on me to return thanks for the meal. Their little three-year-old was sitting in his high chair at the table with us. When I finished, he turned to his mother and said, "What did that man do?" Obviously, they didn't very often give thanks for their meal. The little fellow was completely uninhibited in what he said.

Now a child may be uninhibited, but the church is not to manifest itself as a baby all the time. It is to grow up and develop some inhibitions. There are certain things an adult doesn't say that a little child may say. The church is not to remain in babyhood but is to mature, and God has given to each child of His grace in which to grow.

But unto every one of us is given grace according to the measure of the gift of Christ [Eph. 4:7].

God has given gifts to believers, as we see in Romans 12 and again in 1 Corinthians, chapters 12—14. Although believers are to give diligence to maintain the unity of the Spirit, this does not mean that each is a carbon copy of the other. Each believer is given a gift so that he may function in the body of believers in a particular way. Paul writes, "But the manifestation of the Spirit is given to every man to profit withal" (1 Cor. 12:7). This means that a gift is the Spirit of God doing something through the believer for the purpose of building up the body of believers. It is for the profit of the whole body of believers. No gift is given to you to develop you spiritually. A gift is given to you in order that you might function in the body of believers to benefit and bless the church.

Many folks say, "Dr. McGee, we do not speak in tongues in the church. We do it for our private devotions." I can say to them categorically from the Word of God that they are wrong. Gifts are given to profit the church. No gift is to be used selfishly for personal profit. In fact, it is not a gift if it is being used that way. A gift is given to every member of the body to enable him to function for a very definite reason in his position in the body.

Suppose my eyes would tell me that they are sleepy and will not get up with me. Suppose my legs say they won't carry me downstairs to my study. I need both my eyes and my legs, and I hope my brain cooperates too. In fact, all the members of my body need to work together, each member doing the job it's supposed to do.

Each believer is given a gift so that he may function in the body of believers in a particular way. When he does this, the body functions. That is where we find the unity of the Spirit. Along with the gift it says every one of us is given grace to exercise that gift in the power and fullness of the Spirit of God. When each believer functions in his peculiar gift, it produces a harmony, as does each member of the human body. However, when one member of the body suffers, the whole body suffers. This means, my friend, that if you do not exercise your gift in the body, you throw us all out of tune.

Wherefore he saith, When he ascended up on high, he led captivity captive, and gave gifts unto men [Eph. 4:8].

You will notice that this is a quotation from Psalm 68:18: "Thou hast ascended on high, thou hast led captivity captive: thou hast received gifts for men; yea, for the rebellious also, that the LORD God might dwell among them." Someone may point out that apparently there is a discrepancy here. Ephesians says, "He gave gifts unto men" and the psalm says, "He received gifts for men." Is this a misquote from the Old Testament?

Please note that an author has a right to change his own writings, but nobody else has that right. I was misquoted in an article and the publisher had to apologize for misquoting me. However, I have a right to misquote my own writing if I want to do so, and if it serves my purpose.

In the verse before us the Holy Spirit changes the words, and He does it for a purpose. Back in the Book of Psalms we are told that the Lord Jesus had received gifts for men. He had all the gifts ready. Then He came to earth. Now that He has been here and has gone back to the Father, He is distributing the gifts among men. He is giving them to us through the Holy Spirit. Actually this passage shows again how very accurate the Bible is and that this is not a misquote.

"When he ascended up on high" refers to the ascension of Christ. At that time He did two things: (1) He led captivity captive, which refers, I believe, to the redeemed of the Old Testament who went to paradise when they died. Christ took these believers with Him out of paradise into the very presence of God when He ascended. Today when a believer dies, we are not told that he goes to paradise, but rather he is absent from the body and present with the Lord (see 2 Cor. 5:8; Phil. 1:23). (2) When Christ ascended He also gave gifts to men. This means that He conferred gifts upon living believers in the church so that they might witness to the world. In His ascension, Christ not only brought the Old Testament saints into God's presence, but He also, through the Holy Spirit, bestowed His gifts. At the Day of Pentecost the Holy Spirit baptized believers into the body of Christ and then endowed them with certain gifts, enabling them to function as members of the body. The Holy Spirit put each of them in a certain place in the body, and He has been doing the same with each new believer ever since.

(Now that he ascended, what is it but that he also descended first into the lower parts of the earth?

He that descended is the same also that ascended up far above all heavens, that he might fill all things.) [Eph. 4:9–10].

The logical explanation of these verses is that since Christ ascended, He must have of necessity descended at some previous period. Some see only the Incarnation in this. The early church fathers saw in it the work of Christ in bringing the Old Testament saints out of paradise up to the throne of God. We are told that He descended into hell. It is not necessary, however, to assume that He entered into some form of suffering after His death. His incarnation and death were His humiliation and descent, and they were adequate to bring the redeemed of the Old Testament into the presence of God. That would explain His fullness here. "He that descended is the same also that ascended up far above all heavens, that he might fill all things." I recognize, however, that there are other interpretations.

And he gave some, apostles; and some, prophets; and some, evangelists; and some, pastors and teachers;

For the perfecting of the saints, for the work of the ministry, for the edifying of the body of Christ:

Till we all come in the unity of the faith, and of the knowledge of the Son of God, unto a perfect man, unto the measure of the stature of the fulness of Christ [Eph. 4:11–13].

I translate it this way: "He Himself gave some [as] apostles, and some [as] prophets and some [as] evangelists, and some [as] pastors and teachers." This verse does not refer to the gifts He has given to men, although it is true that it is He who has given the gifts. What Paul is saying here is that Christ takes certain men who have been given certain gifts and He gives them to the church.

Now notice the purpose for which these men are given to the

church: "For the perfecting of the saints, for the work of the ministry, for the edifying of the body of Christ." These gifted men are given to the church that it might be brought to full maturity.

"Till we all attain unto the unity of the faith, and of the full knowledge of the Son of God, unto a full grown man, unto the measure of the stature of the fulness of Christ." This may sound selfish, but I trust it is understood. What is the purpose of the church in the world? It is to complete itself that it might grow up.

"He Himself"—this is very emphatic—it is the Lord Jesus Himself who gives gifted men to perfect the church. The Lord Jesus is the One who has the authority and is the One who bestows gifts.

He gave "some, apostles" to the church. An apostle was a man who had not only seen the resurrected Christ but had also been directly and personally commissioned by Him to be an apostle. He enjoyed a special inspiration. This is why Paul could state: "Paul, an apostle, (not of men, neither by man, but by Jesus Christ, and God the Father, who raised him from the dead;). . . . For I neither received it of man, neither was I taught it, but by the revelation of Jesus Christ" (Gal. 1:1, 12). This office, by virtue of its very nature, has long since disappeared from the church.

He gave "some, prophets." Here, as in other epistles, this has reference to New Testament prophets. They were men who were given, as were the apostles, particular insight into the doctrines of the faith (see Eph. 3:5). They were under the immediate influence and inspiration of the Holy Spirit, which distinguishes them from teachers (see 1 Cor. 12:10). There is no one around today with the office of apostle or prophet in that sense. They themselves passed off the scene long ago, but they are still members of His church. His church exists not only on earth; part of the church is up in heaven with Him. They are part of that host which is in the presence of God. In another sense they are still with us today. Aren't we studying the Epistle to the Ephesians right now? And who wrote it? The apostle Paul, and he is still with us even though he is up in heaven with Christ. He is absent from the body but present with Christ. Yet he is still a member of the church and he is still an apostle to us.

"Some, evangelists." The evangelists were traveling missionaries. Paul was an evangelist. They were not evangelists as we think of them today. There was no committee or organization to set up a campaign. They went into new territory, and they did it all alone with the Spirit of God who went before them.

He also gave, "some, pastors." These men were the shepherds of the flock.

He gave "some, teachers," the men who were to instruct the flock. This is the gift which is mentioned in Romans 12:7; 1 Corinthians 12:28–29; and 1 Timothy 3:2.

God has given all these men to the church so that the church might be brought to full maturation where there will be inhibitions. You see, the church is not to make a "nut" of herself before the world; she is not to appear ignorant before the world. All these men are to prepare the church so that the believers might do the work of ministering and building up the body of Christ.

We call the pastor of a church a minister, but if you are a Christian, you are as much a minister as he is. You don't have to be ordained to be a minister. The pastor has a special gift of teaching the Word of God so that his members, those who are under him, might do the work of the ministry—they are the ones to go out and do the visitation and the witnessing. I am afraid we have the church in reverse today.

At one time Dr. Lewis Sperry Chafer led his own singing and also did the preaching when he started out as an evangelist. A dear lady came to him one night and said, "Dr. Chafer, you're doing too much. You ought not to lead the singing and do the preaching both. Why don't you get someone else to do the preaching?" Well, he was a musician, but he was primarily a great teacher. Teaching was his great gift, and he used it to equip others for the ministry.

At this point let me say that probably no man in the church has all the gifts; so do not expect your pastor or your minister to be all things. Don't take the viewpoint that he has many gifts. His business is to build the members of the church for the work of the ministry.

Here is a little article that appeared in the bulletin of a small church in the East:

For centuries the principal responsibility for evangelism has been borne by the clergy. The laity were neither called to evangelistic activity nor believed it to be their responsibility. One of the most significant developments in the church (possibly the single most important development in recent centuries) is the revival of lay activity and the growing recognition that the layman is called to a ministry no less important than that of the minister. Elton Trueblood has said, "The Reformation has opened up the *Bible* to the common man; a new Reformation will open up the *ministry* to the common man."

I agree with this article wholeheartedly, and I rejoice that today we are seeing laymen becoming more involved. So many young people today, young Christians, are getting involved in doing the witnessing. Now they need teaching. I think the only reason in the world that they listen to me is because they feel that I can teach them. Believers need teaching so that they can do the work of the ministry.

Sometimes folk get excited when they hear another using my materials. I had a call from a lady in Ohio. Apparently a preacher there was doing a pretty good job of imitating me. He was teaching from my book on Ruth and was even using my illustrations. She said, "I think it is terrible, and you ought to stop him." I asked her if he was doing a good job, and she said he was. So I said, "Praise the Lord, I always felt someone would come along who would do it much better than I do it." You see, my business is to try to prepare others to do the work of the ministry.

One minister wrote and said that he wanted to preach a sermon of mine and asked if he could have permission to do that. I replied, "There is only one thing I ask of you. Do it better than I did, brother." Use the material. We are to build up the body of Christ.

I am going to talk to you very frankly. Don't expect your pastor to do it all. He is there to train you that you might do the work of the ministry and that the church might become mature. We are not to act like a bunch of nitwits today. We are to give a good, clear-cut, intelligent witness to the world. I think the greatest sin in the local church today is the ignorance of the man sitting in the pew; he doesn't know the Word of God, and that is a tragedy. I would hate to get into an airplane if the pilot didn't know any more about flying than the average church member knows about Christianity and the Word of God. The plane wouldn't make it—I think it would crash before it got ten feet into the air. That is the condition of the church today. All believers need to be trained in the Word of God so they can do the work of the ministry.

That we henceforth be no more children, tossed to and fro, and carried about with every wind of doctrine, by the sleight of men, and cunning craftiness, whereby they lie in wait to deceive [Eph. 4:14].

"That we henceforth be no more children." We are to have inhibitions. We are not to run around like a bunch of crying babies. You remember that Paul told the church in Corinth that they were carnal and that they were babies in Christ and a disgrace.

We are not (to use my translation) to be "tossed up and down and driven about with every wind of doctrine (teaching)." Notice that Paul does some mixing of metaphors here. He is trying to bring out vividly the danger of a believer continuing as a babe. You wouldn't, for example, put a baby in a plane to pilot it. My little grandson is a smart boy, but he is not that smart. I wouldn't allow him up there; he would crash. If children were in command of a ship, they would be tossed up and down, driven here and there without direction over the vast expanse of sea. They would become discouraged and seasick. They would lose their way. This is a frightful picture of the possible fate of a child of God.

The figure of speech changes again. "By the sleight of men, and cunning craftiness, whereby they lie in wait to deceive." If you sent babes into the gambling den, the sharpies would take them in with their system of error. I wouldn't think of sending my grandson to Las Vegas to play the slot machines! In fact, I wouldn't want him there even if he lived to be a hundred years old.

Christ's purpose in giving men with different gifts to the church is to develop believers from babyhood to full maturity. Teachers are to be pediatricians. I sometimes use the expression that I am primarily a pediatrician, not an obstetrician. The obstetrician brings the baby into the world. I know he has to get up sometimes at one o'clock in the morning to deliver a baby and that he spends many nights at his work, but he is through with the little angel after he is born. He turns him over to the pediatrician, who makes sure he has everything he needs for normal growth. I have been a pediatrician in my ministry and, only secondly, an obstetrician. I feel that I am called to be the pediatrician—that is, to give the saints the Word of God so they can grow.

> **But speaking the truth in love, may grow up into him in all things, which is the head, even Christ:**

> **From whom the whole body fitly joined together and compacted by that which every joint supplieth, according to the effectual working in the measure of every part, maketh increase of the body unto the edifying of itself in love [Eph. 4:15–16].**

Believers are not to remain children, but rather that in "speaking the truth in love, [they] may grow up into him in all things." The believer is to follow the truth in love; that is, he is to love truth, live it, and speak it. Christ is the truth and the believer must sail his little bark of life with everything pointed toward Christ. Christ is his compass and his magnetic pole.

"Which is the head, even Christ: from whom the whole body fitly joined together and compacted." The body of believers is compared to the physical body and is called the body of Christ.

The body not only receives orders from the Head, who is Christ, but also spiritual nutriment. This produces a harmony where each member is functioning in his place as he receives spiritual supplies from the Head. Also the body has an inward dynamic whereby it renews itself. Likewise the spiritual body is to renew itself in love.

THE PROHIBITION OF THE NEW MAN

This I say therefore, and testify in the Lord, that ye henceforth walk not as other Gentiles walk, in the vanity of their mind,

Having the understanding darkened, being alienated from the life of God through the ignorance that is in them, because of the blindness of their heart:

Who being past feeling have given themselves over unto lasciviousness, to work all uncleanness with greediness [Eph. 4:17–19].

We have seen the *exhibition* of the new man and the *inhibition* of the new man. Now we come to the *prohibition* of the new man. There is the negative side of the believer's life, which I think is important for us to see. There is not enough emphasis on it. We talk about "new morality" which is nothing in the world but old sin. There is a liberty in Christ, but it is not a license to sin.

Scriptural prohibitions for the new man are different from some of the prohibitions that people set up. I can't find, for example, where it says that women should not wear makeup. I know a group who for years judged the spirituality of women by the amount of makeup they wore. I've also seen young girls who thought they were spiritual because they had disheveled hair and no makeup on, and actually they looked like walking zombies. Christians should do the best they can with what they have. That doesn't mean, of course, that they should be painted up like a barber pole. However, some Christians insist upon a number of these man-made prohibitions which are not found in Scripture.

God's prohibitions for the new man are the negatives of His Word. We have had too much on the power of positive thinking today. We need a little of the power of negative thinking. Have you ever thought that in the Garden of Eden the primary command was a negative command? "But of the tree of the knowledge of good and evil, thou shalt not eat of it: for in the day that thou eatest thereof thou shalt surely die" (Gen. 2:17). Then you come to the Ten Commandments. They are very negative but also very good. Now here in Ephesians we see some negative thinking, some prohibitions for the child of God. We are not to walk "as other Gentiles walk." This is the negative side.

Paul returns at this juncture to the practical aspect of the believer's walk. He had introduced it in verses 1–3, but he was detoured by the introduction of the subject of the unity of the church. Now he gives a picture of the lives of Gentiles and the lives of the Ephesians before their conversion. Remember in chapter 2, verses 11–12, he told how they had been far off, strangers without hope and without God, living in sin. That was their picture.

This is still a graphic picture of the lost man today. Paul gives four aspects of the walk of the Gentiles which illustrate the absolute futility and insane purpose of the life of the lost man.

"In the vanity of their mind" means the empty illusion of the life that thinks there is satisfaction in sin. Oh, how many people walk that way! I feel so sorry for these young people who have been taken in by the promoters of immorality as a life style. A girl told me that she had had two abortions—murdered two babies, and was not married—what a life! That is not the life of happiness that God has planned for His children, my friend. It is the walk of a lost person, walking in the vanity of the mind. It is an empty illusion of life.

Drinking cocktails is another illusion. Alcoholism takes its toll. An alcoholic woman has started listening to our Bible teaching program and is now fighting a battle to be delivered from alcohol. She says, "Oh, it seemed so smart, so sophisticated to drink cocktails!" How tragic.

"Having the understanding darkened" means that the lost man has lost his perception of moral values. That is exactly what is being promoted in our day—a loss of perception of moral values.

"Being alienated from the life of God through the ignorance that is in them" is a picture of all mankind without Christ. It is the rebellion of Adam which is inherited by all his children. What a picture it is of a man today. He thinks he is living. One man told me he spent a week's wages for one evening in a nightclub. What for? To try to have a good time. That's an expensive way to try to have fun. He was alienated from the life of God; he had no communication with God: he was dead in trespasses and sin. Such a man is ignorant of the inestimable advantage of a relationship with God. The result is a hardening of the heart.

"Who being past feeling have given themselves over unto lasciviousness [which is uncleanness], to work all uncleanness with greediness [or covetousness]." Their continuance in this state of moral ineptitude brings them down to the level where they have no feeling of wrongdoing. There are a lot of folk like that today. They are apathetic. The resultant condition is to plunge further into immorality and lasciviousness. This vicious cycle leads to a desire to go even deeper into sin. If you paint the town red tonight, you have to have a bigger bucket and a bigger brush for tomorrow night. The meaning here is to covet the very depths of immorality. Men in sin are never satisfied with sin. They become abandoned to sin. This is what it means in chapter 1 of Romans that God gave them up to all uncleanness through their own lusts. You can reach the place, my friend, where you are an abandoned sinner.

But ye have not so learned Christ:

If so be that ye have heard him, and have been taught by him, as the truth is in Jesus [Eph. 4:20–21].

Here is the contrast with the life of the Gentiles. If anyone is not listening to Jesus, then Jesus must not be his Savior. The Lord Jesus is the Shepherd and His sheep hear His voice. If you haven't heard His voice, then you are not one of His sheep.

What will change the Gentiles from their old nature? What are they to do? They are to listen to Christ. They are to hear Him. They are to be taught by Him. Those who are not His sheep will not hear Him.

When an unsaved man writes to me and says that he disagrees with me, I am not upset. I think, *Fine, I hope you don't agree with me.* Something would be wrong if he did agree. The saved person looks to the Lord Jesus as his Shepherd. He listens to the Shepherd and he follows Him. The unsaved person goes his own way.

"The truth is in Jesus." Although His life on earth cannot be imitated by anyone, the very life of Jesus is an example to the believer. Jesus is the One who has been the pioneer; He is the example of life here on earth. He is the One who also went through the doorway of death for us. There is no reason for any believer to be in the dark today or to be ignorant or to be blind.

> **That ye put off concerning the former conversation the old man, which is corrupt according to the deceitful lusts;**
>
> **And be renewed in the spirit of your mind;**
>
> **And that ye put on the new man, which after God is created in righteousness and true holiness [Eph. 4:22–24].**

"That ye put off concerning . . . the old man . . . and that ye put on the new man." We are to put off the old man and put on the new man in the same manner that we change our clothes. It is like putting off an old and unclean garment and then putting on a garment that is new and clean. The putting off the old man and putting on the new man cannot be done by self-effort, nor can it be done by striving to imitate Christ's conduct. It has been done *for* the believing sinner by the death of Christ. We are like babes who cannot dress themselves. I have learned with my little grandson that a child doesn't do very well when he tries to dress himself. As Christians we never reach the place where we can do that, and we don't need to try. It already has been done for us. We are told in the Epistle to the Romans that the old man has already been crucified in the death of Christ. "Knowing this, that our old man is crucified with him, that the body of sin might be destroyed, that henceforth we should not serve sin" (Rom. 6:6). In view of the truth that the old man has already been crucified with Christ, we are to put it off in the power of the Holy Spirit. This does not mean that the flesh, the old nature, is ever eliminated in this life. We do not get rid of the old nature, but we are not to live in it; that is, we are not to allow it to control our lives.

On the other hand, we do have a new nature. This is the result of regeneration by the Holy Spirit. Any man in Christ is a new creature. We are to live in that new nature, that new man. This is a repetition of the great message of Romans.

"Which after God is created in righteousness and true holiness." This shows that this is the imputed righteousness of Christ, and that all is to be done consistent with the holy character of God. Since we have been declared righteous and we are in Christ seated in the heavenlies, our walk down here should be commensurate with our position.

> **Wherefore putting away lying, speak every man truth with his neighbour: for we are members one of another.**
>
> **Be ye angry, and sin not: let not the sun go down upon your wrath:**
>
> **Neither give place to the devil [Eph. 4:25–27].**

Paul returns to the prohibitions which he began in verse 17. The believer is told to walk no longer as the Gentiles walk. These injunctions continue through the remainder of the epistle.

"Speak every man truth" is the injunction that leads all the rest. When the old man was put off in the crucifixion of Christ, the lying tongue and deceitful heart were put on the cross. One of the reasons Jesus had to die for us was because you and I are liars. We ought always to speak the truth. David said, "I said in my haste, All men are liars" (Ps. 116:11). I remember hearing Dr. W. I. Carroll quote this years ago. He pointed out that David said he thought this "in his haste." Dr. Carroll remarked, "I've had a long time to think it over, and I still agree with David."

Speaking the truth would resolve most of the problems in the average church. Long ago I gave up the idea of trying to straighten out all of the lies that I hear in Christian circles. I found out that I could spend all my time doing that. Since believers are members of one body, speaking the truth is imperative.

Chrysostom drew this ridiculous analogy but it does illustrate the truth:

> Let not the eye lie to the foot, nor the foot to the eye. If there be a deep pit and its mouth covered with reeds shall present to the eye the appearance of solid ground, will not the eye use the foot to ascertain whether it is hollow underneath, or whether it is firm and resists? Will the foot tell a lie, and not the truth as it is? And what, again, if the eye were to spy a serpent or a wild beast, will it lie to the foot?

The feet wouldn't deceive the eyes because they are members of the same body. Neither would the eye deceive the feet. So in the church there ought to be honesty and truth among the members.

"Be ye angry, and sin not." The believer is commanded to be angered with certain conditions and with certain people. There seems to be an idea today that a Christian is one who is a "blah," that he is sweet under all circumstances and conditions. Will you hear me carefully? No believer can be neutral in the battle of truth. He should hate the lying and gossiping tongue, especially of another Christian. However, we should not hate or loathe the person with an innate hatred or malice, as Peter calls it. Malice is something that should not be in the life of the believer. "Wherefore laying aside all malice . . ." (1 Pet. 2:1). Malice has been described as congealed anger. When the wrong is corrected, there should be no animosity. Forgive and forget is the principle. Harboring hatred and sinful feelings gives the devil an advantage in our lives. Many people have certain hang-ups. They hate certain people—they can't get over it and can't forgive. My friend, we should forgive and forget if the person is willing to give up his lying.

The Lord Jesus showed anger. He went into the synagogue, and there was a man with a withered hand. What angered Him was that the Pharisees had planted that man there just to see what He would do. "And when he had looked round about on them with anger, being grieved for the hardness of their hearts, he saith unto the man, Stretch forth thine hand. And he stretched it out: and his hand was restored whole as the other" (Mark 3:5). Our Lord was *angry* at the Pharisees for doing such a thing. Also we are told that God is angry all day long with the wicked, but that the minute they give up their wickedness and turn to Him, He will save them. That should be the attitude of the believer.

I heard of a custodian who had remained in a church which had had lots of problems. There was trouble, bitterness, hatred, and little cliques in the church. They had had one pastor after another, but the custodian remained through the years. A visitor who knew about the church asked him how he had been able to stay so long under such circumstances. He replied, "I just got into neutral and let them push me around." A great many people think that that is being a Christian. May I say to you that no Christian can be neutral. We are in a great battle, as we shall see later in this epistle.

Let him that stole steal no more: but rather let him labour, working with his hands the thing which is good, that he may have to give to him that needeth.

Let no corrupt communication proceed out of your mouth, but that which is good to the use of edifying, that it may minister grace unto the hearers [Eph. 4:28–29].

"Let him that stole steal no more." Man by his sinful nature is a thief as well as a liar. When I was a boy, I ran around with a mean gang of boys—I was the only good boy in the crowd, of course. During watermelon season, we stole watermelons. The farmer might have given us one out of his patch, but they tasted better if we swiped them. We also stole peaches and apples from the orchards. And in the wintertime we would steal eggs and take them down to Old Buzzard Creek and roast them. There wasn't anything that was safe from us.

After I was converted, I still had this impulse. In fact, once I was going to visit a man who had a marvelous watermelon patch by the side of a country road. I was so tempted to take one of his watermelons that I actually stopped and got out of the car. Then I thought, "Wait a minute. I am going to see the man in a few minutes. He'll give me one. There's no reason for me to do this." I got back in the car and drove off. When I told him my experience, he laughed. "You know," he said, "I might have shot you if you had gone into that watermelon patch. I've had a lot of thieves in there stealing my watermelons, and they are pretty valuable today." Stealing is in our hearts. We are just naturally that way. Paul says here that we are to steal no more, even when it may look as if it is all right.

"But rather let him labour, working with his hands the thing which is good, that he may have to give to him that needeth." The believer is not to get rich for his own selfish ends. Rather, he is to help others with whatever he has that is surplus. Today there are many fine Christian ministries that lag and wilt for lack of funds. Why? Because many believers are accumulating riches for themselves and are not giving as they should give.

"Corrupt communication" means filthy speech—that which is rotten or putrid. An uncontrolled tongue in the mouth of a believer is the index of a corrupt life. Believers who use the shady or questionable story reveal a heart of wickedness. What is in the well of the heart will come up through the bucket of the mouth. The speech of the believer should be on the high plane of instructing and communicating encouragement to other believers. You can have fun and enjoy life— humor has its place—but our humor should not be dirty or filthy.

And grieve not the holy Spirit of God, whereby ye are sealed unto the day of redemption [Eph. 4:30].

"Grieve not the holy Spirit of God." The Holy Spirit is a person who can be grieved. What is it that grieves Him? It is the offenses that have been listed. When a Christian lies, it grieves the Holy Spirit. When a Christian has dirty thoughts, it grieves the Holy Spirit. What happens when any person is grieved? It breaks the fellowship. The Holy Spirit cannot work in your life when you have grieved Him, when fellowship with Him has been broken.

"Whereby ye are sealed"—this tells us that we can grieve the Holy Spirit, but we cannot grieve Him *away*, because we are sealed in Him.

How wonderful this is! You were sealed in the Holy Spirit at the moment of regeneration.

"Unto the day of redemption"—He seals you until the day when He will present you to the Lord Jesus Christ. A believer cannot unseal His work which continues to the day of redemption, but the believer may grieve Him. What is the great difference between Christians today? The real difference is that some Christians live with a grieved Holy Spirit and some live with an ungrieved Holy Spirit.

> **Let all bitterness, and wrath, and anger, and clamour, and evil speaking, be put away from you, with all malice:**
>
> **And be ye kind one to another, tenderhearted, forgiving one another, even as God for Christ's sake hath forgiven you [Eph. 4:31–32].**

These last two verses are in sharp contrast one with the other. There is an additional listing of that which grieves the Holy Spirit in verse 31—these are sins of the emotional nature. Instead, the emotional responses, which God wants us to have, are given in verse 32.

"Bitterness" is an irritable state of mind which produces harsh and hard opinions of others. Someone once came up to me and told me what he thought of another Christian. A third Christian who was present later said, "Don't put too much stress on what he said, Dr. McGee, because he is bitter." A great many people are speaking out of bitterness, and when they do, it hurts. This grieves the Holy Spirit.

"Wrath, and anger" are outbursts of passion. Bishop Moule makes this distinction between them, "Wrath denotes rather the *acute* passion, and the other the *chronic*."

"Clamour" means the bold assertion of supposed rights and grievances. There are people in the church who feel that the pastor isn't paying attention to them if he doesn't shake their hand. Sometimes they even become bitter and clamorous over a supposed slight. Who can say that the pastor must run around and shake hands with everyone simply to keep people happy? It is this kind of attitude that grieves the Holy Spirit.

"Evil speaking" is blasphemy, but it also means all kinds of slander; and "malice," as we have noted before, is congealed hatred.

"Be put away from you." All these sins are to be put away or, literally, taken away. In the Greek it is an aorist imperative, requiring a one-time decisive act if the Holy Spirit is not to be grieved. We must make a decision to put these sins away.

Now comes a marked contrast. "Be (become) ye" denotes the radical change that should take place in the believer so that there will be no vacuum in his life.

"Kind one to another" means Christian courtesy. "Tenderhearted" is a more intense word than kind. It means to be full of deep and mellow affection. Some believers are like that—they are wonderful friends. When they see you, they put their arms around you. I went to college and then to seminary with a fellow and then helped him in meetings for years. He is retired now. When we saw each other in Florida some time back, we just flung our arms around each other. We were tenderhearted toward one another—we love each other in the Lord.

"Forgiving one another" is a reflexive form of phrase. It is literally, "forgiving one another yourselves." It means to give and take in a relation to the faults of one another. We are to forgive rather than magnify the faults of others.

"Even as God for Christ's sake hath forgiven you." All of this is to be done on a twofold basis. First, this conduct will not grieve the Holy Spirit. Second, the basis of forgiveness is not legal, but gracious. This is not a command under law but is on the basis of the grace of God exhibited in our forgiveness because Christ died for us. We are to forgive because we have been forgiven. It is not that we forgive in order to get forgiveness. Note the contrast: Christ was stating the *legal* grounds for forgiveness in the Sermon on the Mount when He said, "For if ye forgive men their trespasses, your heavenly Father will also forgive you: but if ye forgive not men their trespasses, neither will your Father forgive your trespasses" (Matt. 6:14–15). Here in Ephesians we are told to forgive on the basis of the *grace* of God which He exhibited in our forgiveness for Christ's sake, because Christ died for us. This is quite wonderful!

CHAPTER 5

THEME: The church *will be a* bride; *the engagement of the church; the experience of the church; the expectation of the church*

There is really a mixing of metaphors here. In chapter 4 the church is called a new man, and now the church is to be a bride. The emphasis of this chapter is on the future—the church *will* be a bride. The church is not a bride today. The church is a new man walking in the world, and the church is espoused (engaged) to Christ but is not yet wedded to Him. The wedding hasn't taken place yet. The church will be a bride with Christ after the Rapture. "And I John saw the holy city, new Jerusalem, coming down from God out of heaven, prepared as a bride adorned for her husband. . . . And there came unto me one of the seven angels which had the seven vials full of the seven last plagues, and talked with me, saying, Come hither, I will shew thee the bride, the Lamb's wife" (Rev. 21:2, 9).

On this earth we are to walk as a future bride. We are engaged now. This is what Paul wrote to the Corinthians: ". . . for I have espoused you to one husband, that I may present you as a chaste virgin to Christ" (2 Cor. 11:2). When a girl is engaged and preparing for her wedding, she doesn't have time for her old boyfriends. She won't be going out with Tom tonight and with Dick tomorrow night and with Harry the following night. She is engaged, and she has no interest in them anymore. How can we who are engaged to Christ live as the world lives? We are going to be presented to Christ someday. We are going to live with Him throughout eternity, and He is going to be our Lord and our Master.

THE ENGAGEMENT OF THE CHURCH

Be ye therefore followers of God, as dear children;

And walk in love, as Christ also hath loved us, and hath given himself for us an offering and a sacrifice to God for a sweet-smelling savour [Eph. 5:1–2].

"Therefore" connects this section with the preceding where the walk of the believer is under consideration and continues the injunctions for Christian conduct. These injunctions have a definite bearing upon the church which will be presented to Christ without spot or blemish. Such a high and lofty goal, which is entirely the work of Christ, is a compelling dynamic for chaste conduct here and now.

We have learned that the Holy Spirit indwells every believer and seals every believer, but that we can grieve the Holy Spirit. If we engage in those things mentioned in chapter 4, verse 31, it means we will grieve the Holy Spirit—but it does not mean that we are no longer children of God. It does mean that the unsaved world won't believe that we are the children of God. We are, however, sealed by the Spirit of God until the day of redemption, the day when the Spirit of God will present the church to the Lord Jesus. This goal should lead us to chaste conduct.

The believer is to be an imitator of God, especially in the matter of forgiveness. However, this applies to all aspects of the Christian walk. The Gentiles who formerly walked on a very low plane are now lifted to the high level of love. They are now called "dear children" or beloved children. The plane of love to which they are lifted is the love which Christ exhibited when He loved us enough to give Himself as an offering and a sacrifice for us.

"And hath given himself for us an offering and a sacrifice to God for a sweet-smelling savour" is a clear-cut reference to the Cross. It makes the death of Christ more than the public execution of a criminal. The Cross was the brazen altar where the Lamb of God was offered as the burnt sacrifice. That sacrifice takes away the sin of the world. It identifies Christ with every sacrifice that was offered in the Old Testament by God's command. They all pointed to Him.

It is in view of the substitutionary, vicarious death of Christ upon the Cross that the believer is to attain to such an exalted plane of love. The believer cannot walk with a grieved Holy Spirit, for only the Spirit can bring forth this fruit in the life. Remember that love is first on the list of the fruit of the Spirit in Galatians 5:22.

But fornication, and all uncleanness, or covetousness, let it not be once named among you, as becometh saints;

Neither filthiness, nor foolish talking, nor jesting, which are not convenient: but rather giving of thanks [Eph. 5:3–4].

The sins described here are those which are prevalent among unbelievers. These are the common sins in the world today. All of them have to do with low forms of immorality. Paul is saying that the child of God cannot habitually engage in these. Even a slight indulgence brings about a revulsion and agony of soul. I have made this statement many times, and I repeat it again: If you can get into sin and not be troubled or bothered by it, you are not a child of God. I do not think there is any other alternative. But if there is conviction in your heart, you can rise and go to your Father as the prodigal son did. You are a son of the Father, and only sons want to go to the Father's house. I have never heard of a pig that wanted to go there. The sins listed here are low sins which characterize the ungodly person.

When you as a believer go to God to confess your sins, you don't just bundle them up and hand the bundle to God. It is not a wholesale affair. Rather, you spell out each sin to Him. For example, if you have a biting tongue and are a gossip who hurts people, tell Him *that* is your sin. When you go to God in confession and name the specific sin, it restores fellowship with Him. These sins are sins that believers drop into sometimes. When they do, they are to confess them to God. Fénelon puts it like this:

Tell God all that is in your heart, as one unloads one's heart, its pleasures and its pains, to a dear friend. Tell Him your troubles, that He may comfort you; tell Him your joys, that He may sober them; tell Him your longings, that He may purify them; tell Him your dislikes, that He may help you to conquer them; talk to Him of your temptations, that He may shield you from them; show Him the wounds of your heart, that He may heal them; lay bare your indifference to good, your depraved tastes for evil, your instability. Tell Him how self-love makes you unjust to others, how vanity tempts you to be insincere, how pride disguises you to yourself as to others.

If you thus pour out all your weaknesses, needs, troubles, there will be no lack of what to say. You will never exhaust the subject. It is continually being renewed. People who have no secrets from each other never want for subjects of conversation. They do not weigh their words, for there is nothing to be held back; neither do they seek for something to say. They talk out of the abundance of the heart, without consideration, just what they think. Blessed are they who attain to such familiar, unreserved intercourse with God.

The great need of all believers is to go to God and tell Him what is really in our hearts. Someone may say, "It is just unbelievable that Christians would even commit such sins as are listed here." Friend, if you had been a pastor as long as I have, you would know that they do fall into these sins. Many Christian people feel that they have committed an unpardonable sin, but they have not. There *is* a way back to God!

"Fornication" is accepted by the world as a norm of conduct. It is a sin that is looked upon as not being very bad. When the gross immorality of the hour started creeping in, it was called the *new* morality. Some time ago many of us were shocked when we heard that in the college dormitories the boys and girls were in the same building but on different floors. Now it has changed so that boys and girls are roommates. When I went to college, the boys could visit in the living room of the girls' dormitory. And I still think that is the best way to do it. I'll stick with the Bible. Fornication is a sin. Regardless of where you are or who you are, if you are living in fornication today, you cannot be a child of God. Someone may say, "Wait a minute. You said a child of God could confess a sin and come back into fellowship with God." That is right, but a child of God cannot confess a sin and then persist in *living in* that sin. That is a dead giveaway that such a person is not a child of God.

"All uncleanness" includes all forms of immorality. "Covetousness" is a grasping desire—and not just for money or material wealth. It may be a desire to be mentally superior to someone else. It could be coveting a home or a position. Some people love to be president of something. Of course, it also includes the covetousness for money. It has been said that the miser thinks dollars are flat so he can stack them, and the prodigal thinks they are round so he can roll them. Whether one stacks them or spends them, covetousness means gaining everything for your own selfish ends.

Some people try to garner together all the honors of this world. I know ministers who would never be guilty of trying to get rich, but they surely are after position. They want a position in their denomination or in their community. Covetousness is a rotten sin that is in our old natures.

"Let it not be once named among you." This means they are not to be spoken of with approval or desire. Obviously, I am naming these sins with neither approval nor desire.

"Filthiness" speaks of the utmost in depravity. These are the low-down, dirty things one hears today.

"Foolish talking" means to gloat or brag about sinning. Have you ever heard men or even women boast about how much they drank at a party? Have you heard them boast of their conquests in the realm of sex? That is foolish talking.

"Jesting" does not mean good, clean humor—I'd be guilty of jesting if it meant that. Jesting means to make light of sensuality and immorality. It means telling dirty stories.

"But rather giving of thanks" is to be the context of Christian conversation. I would often play golf with a very wonderful Christian layman whom I loved in the Lord. Sometimes an unsaved man would join us. He would make a few bad shots, and then he would lose his temper. He would ask God to damn the golf course, the sand traps, his golf clubs, and anything else he could think of. My friend would always say, "Praise the Lord, bless the Lord." The unbeliever would ask, "Why do you say that?" The Christian would ask, "Why do you take God's name in vain?" The reply would be, "It's a habit." "It's also a habit with me," my friend would say. "Every time I hear a man ask

God to damn something, I praise and thank Him for something. I sort of want to balance the budget down here." On several occasions that stopped the cussing. And it is good for us as Christians to make a habit of giving thanks.

For this ye know, that no whoremonger, nor unclean person, nor covetous man, who is an idolater, hath any inheritance in the kingdom of Christ and of God [Eph. 5:5].

It is clearly understood that the unregenerate man who practices these sins has no portion in the kingdom of Christ and God. If a professing Christian practices these sins, he immediately classifies himself. No matter what his testimony may be on Sunday or what position he may have in the church, such a person is saying to the lost world that he is not a child of God. To *live* in the corruption of the flesh is to place one's self beyond the pale of a child of God.

Let no man deceive you with vain words: for because of these things cometh the wrath of God upon the children of disobedience.

Be not ye therefore partakers with them [Eph. 5:6-7].

In view of the fact that the wrath of God will be poured out on the unregenerate because of these sins, it follows that the child of God cannot participate in them without incurring the displeasure and judgment of God. If such a person is really a child of God, God will judge him. He judged David, you may recall. When David slipped into sin, God put the lash on his back and never took it off. "For if we would judge ourselves, we should not be judged. But when we are judged, we are chastened of the Lord, that we should not be condemned with the world" (1 Cor. 11:31-32).

If you can sin and get by with it, you are not a child of God. Do you know why? Because God would have to condemn you with the world, which would mean that you are not saved. If you are a child of God and do these things, God will chasten you—He will take you to the woodshed right here and now. If God doesn't chasten you, you are in a frightful condition. It means you are not His child, because God does not spank the devil's children.

For ye were sometimes darkness, but now are ye light in the Lord: walk as children of light:

(For the fruit of the Spirit is in all goodness and righteousness and truth;)

Proving what is acceptable unto the Lord [Eph. 5:8–10].

Paul reminds the believers of their former state prior to conversion. They were not just *in* darkness, they *were* darkness. We speak of the unregenerate as being in darkness, but it is worse than that. When I went alone to play golf on one occasion, I was teamed up with a man who was unsaved—in fact, he was a bartender. As he talked, I realized that he was not only *in* darkness, he *was* darkness. My, what a life that man had!

"Now are ye light in the Lord," which means we are to reflect Him who is the Light of the world. Paul identifies the fruit of light. He marks out those characteristics which always accompany light: "In all goodness," which means kindness; "righteousness," meaning moral rectitude; and "truth," referring primarily to sincerity and genuineness. The believer is to prove or test his life in this manner to see if he is in the will of God and therefore well-pleasing to Him.

You will remember that 1 John 1:7 speaks of walking in the light as He is in the light. Someone asked me what it means to walk in the light of God. Here we have a description of it from the Word of God: walk in kindness, in goodness, in righteousness (moral rectitude), and in truth, which is sincerity and genuineness. And this is to be our walk seven days a week—not only on Sunday. And it means twenty-four hours of those seven days and sixty minutes of every hour.

And have no fellowship with the unfruitful works of darkness, but rather reprove them.

> For it is a shame even to speak of those things which are
> done of them in secret.
>
> But all things that are reproved are made manifest by
> the light: for whatsoever doth make manifest is light
> [Eph. 5:11–13].

We are to "have no fellowship with the unfruitful works of darkness."
A child of God simply cannot go along with the "works of darkness"
as light and darkness cannot mingle in the physical world. For the
things done in secret by them are even shameful to speak of. We are
not even to talk about them.

Rather, we are to "reprove" or convict them. This does not mean
that the believer is to become a reformer. It does mean that by the light
of his life he is a rebuke to the works of darkness. Light reveals what
the darkness conceals. Darkness is not driven away by preaching at it;
darkness is dissipated by the presence of light.

There are too many Christians who take the critical method or the
preaching method. They try to correct an unsaved person by saying,
"You shouldn't be doing that." My friend, that is not the way to approach the darkness. You are to be light. You cannot preach to people
about these things. You cannot tell them what to do and not to do. I
constantly get letters from people who are telling me that I should
preach against certain sins. No, my business is to turn on the light of
the Word of God—that which God calls right. You see, you are not able
to win a person to Christ by lecturing to him and telling him what is
wrong. You are not to try to get the unsaved man to change his conduct; he *cannot* change his conduct. He needs to be born again in
order to change. You are not to shake your finger under his nose and
say, "Don't do that. Don't be a bad boy." You are to be light, and light
will always affect darkness.

I remember a very dear lady in my congregation when I was a pastor in downtown Los Angeles. She was a dominant character, however. She came to me and told me that her husband was unsaved and
asked me to remember him in prayer. I did so faithfully. Then she
came to me and told me that he was coming to church but would never

accept the invitation to receive Christ as his Savior. Then she told me this: "At breakfast I talk to him with tears about receiving Christ. Again at dinner I talk to him and cry." I got to thinking what it would be like to have two meals a day with a crying woman. So I told her absolutely never to mention the subject to him again. She should fix him the nicest meals possible and be the sweetest person she knew how to be. "Oh," she said, "that wouldn't work. We are supposed to witness." You see, she didn't really understand what it meant to be a witness. Anyway, she did try the plan. She quit blubbering in his presence, and she stopped lecturing to him. In less than six months that man made a decision for Christ. He had been listening to the wrong preacher before that. She had been preaching to him when she should have been a light. Remember that darkness is not dissipated by lecturing or by preaching. Darkness is dissipated by light.

> **Wherefore he saith, Awake thou that sleepest, and arise from the dead, and Christ shall give thee light [Eph. 5:14].**

Here is a command which is humanly impossible to obey. How can a person awake from the dead? How can a person awake out of spiritual death? Only God can awaken us. I think what Paul means here is that the believers who have fallen into a spiritual stupor are to wake up.

> **See then that ye walk circumspectly, not as fools, but as wise,**
>
> **Redeeming the time, because the days are evil.**
>
> **Wherefore be ye not unwise, but understanding what the will of the Lord is [Eph. 5:15–17].**

My own translation is: "Look carefully how ye walk, not as unwise, but be as wise men, buying up the time, because the days are evil. On this account become not senseless (foolish) but understanding (being prudent) what the will of the Lord is." This is another injunction regarding the walk of the believer. He is to walk wisely. His walk is to reveal the urgency of the hour and the importance of living for God. The entire objective in his walk is to stay in the will of God. He walks in the will of God as a train runs on the track. His walk in this world demonstrates that he belongs to Christ.

When you walk into a place of business, you will find the salesman in there on his toes: he is dynamic. If a man is a child of God, how does he act when he is not in his place of business trying to make a dollar? Is he on his toes? Is he dynamic? Is he living for God? The believer is to walk in this world as though he belonged to Christ.

There is a saying that you never ask a Texan if he is a Texan. If he is a Texan, he'll let you know it without your asking. If he is not a Texan, you wouldn't want to embarrass him! My friend, a Christian ought to walk in such a way that you know he is a child of God without asking him. We all need to look carefully how we walk.

THE EXPERIENCE OF THE CHURCH

Each real believer should have an experience—I believe in experience. Now notice what is to be his experience:

And be not drunk with wine, wherein is excess; but be filled with the Spirit;

Speaking to yourselves in psalms and hymns and spiritual songs, singing and making melody in your heart to the Lord [Eph. 5:18–19].

My translation puts it like this: "Be not made drunk with wine in which is riot (dissoluteness), but be filled with the Spirit; speaking one to another in psalms and hymns and spiritual songs, singing and making melody in your heart to the Lord." This is not just a dry discourse against the evils of drunkenness, even though drunkenness was the besetting sin of the ancient world—and it is still the besetting sin of the hour. It may actually be the sin that will destroy America. But this is not a lecture on drunkenness. Actually, Paul is making a comparison. Don't be drunk with wine. Why not? Because it will stimulate temporarily: it will energize the flesh, but then it will let you down and lead you in the direction of profligacy and dissoluteness and will finally eventuate in desperation and despair and delirium tremens. That is not what you need. Now it is true that people today feel a need for something, which I think explains the cocktail hour and the barroom. They turn to hard liquor to fill that need. If they are not children of God, they have no other resource or recourse. However, the child of God is to be filled with the Holy Spirit. This is to be the *experience* of the believer.

What does it mean to be filled with the Holy Spirit? We can find the analogy in the man who is drinking, which is the reason Paul uses it here. The man who is drinking is possessed by the wine. You can tell that a man is drunk. In contrast, it is the Holy Spirit who should be the One to possess the believer. It is a divine intoxication that is to fill that need. This is not an excessive emotionalism but that which furnishes the dynamic for living and for accomplishing something for God. When we are filled by the Holy Spirit, it means that we are *controlled* by the Holy Spirit.

The walk of the believer and his being filled with the Spirit are closely related. Paul says a believer is to walk carefully and "circumspectly" and "be filled with the Spirit." These are commands which are given to the believer. This filling is a constant renewal of the believer's life for strength and action, which is indicated here by the use of the present tense. The Spirit-filled believer not only walks wisely, but his Christian character is evidenced by the fruit of the Spirit (see Gal. 5:22–23).

A believer is never commanded to be baptized with the Holy Spirit, but we *are* told that we are "baptized into one body . . ." (1 Cor. 12:13). Did we do that by some effort on our part? No, it was by our faith in Jesus Christ. The Holy Spirit regenerates and indwells us. The Holy Spirit seals us, and the Holy Spirit baptizes us and puts us into the body of believers.

However, the believer needs the filling of the Spirit to serve Christ. The disciples were gathered on the Day of Pentecost. They needed to go out into the world for Christ, and they were filled with the Spirit. They had that experience which enabled them to witness on that day.

To be filled with the Spirit is, I think, as simple as driving to a filling station and saying, "Fill it up." As I start out in the morning with the Lord I say, "Lord, I want to walk today in the Spirit. I cannot do it myself. I need Your power. I need Your help." We as believers need to start the day by asking for an infilling of the Holy Spirit. This is something which is desperately needed by believers.

You may have been filled with the Spirit yesterday or last week, but that won't suffice for today. I buy gasoline from a friend of mine who runs the station. I got my tank filled up one morning, and the next morning I was back again and said, "Fill 'er up." He asked, "Where in the world have you been?" So I told him that I had been down to Yucca Valley, where I had spoken at a sunrise service and then a church service. You see, friend, when you are filled with the Spirit, you will do something for God; you will be walking in the Spirit. But that doesn't mean you will have enough for tomorrow. You need another infilling for tomorrow. The old gas tank needs another fill up.

This is the reason some people can be so mightily used of God one day and feel so empty the next. I have had that feeling, and I'm sure you have. We need a fresh infilling of the Holy Spirit. This will enable us to walk in the Spirit. We may stumble and fall at times. My little grandson is learning to walk and right now he has a bruised spot on his forehead and on his nose. But he gets up and tries again and someday he will be a good walker. God wants you and me to learn to walk in the Spirit. He wants us to be filled with the Spirit.

Now what is one of the evidences of being filled with the Holy Spirit? It is "speaking to yourselves in psalms and hymns and spiritual songs, singing and making melody in your heart to the Lord." It is a good thing that the Spirit of God said it was *speaking* one to another. If He had said *singing*, it would have left me out. I think "psalms" refers to the Book of Psalms, as probably all of them had been set to music. "Hymns" were composed by men to glorify God. They were on a very high plane. The "spiritual songs" were less formal than either psalms or hymns. Probably some of them were composed as the person was singing. This is the manifestation of the infilling of the Spirit because He brings joy into the life of the believer.

I'd like to mention one more thing about the comparison of being drunk with wine and being filled with the Spirit. I notice in motels and hotels where we stay as we go across the country that they have what they call the "happy hour" or the "attitude adjustment hour" or something else. Around five o'clock people go in, sit on a bar stool and drink so they will be sociable by six or seven and fit to live with for awhile. I have watched people go into those places, and they didn't look happy when they went in, but neither did they look happy when they came out.

Now, believers need an attitude adjustment, but they don't need the spirits that come from a bottle; they need to be filled with the Holy Spirit so that they might radiate the joy of the Lord. The apostle John says that one of the reasons he wrote his epistle was so that "your joy may be full" (see John 15:11). This fullness of joy is to be through our fellowship with the Father and with Jesus Christ (see 1 John 1:3-4). We ought to have a good time and we ought to have fun in the church—I don't mean a period of silliness—but the joy of the Lord should be there. That kind of joy comes through the filling of the Holy Spirit.

Giving thanks always for all things unto God and the Father in the name of our Lord Jesus Christ [Eph. 5:20].

Another evidence of being filled with the Spirit is an attitude of thankfulness. We note in the Book of Psalms a great amount of thanksgiving and praise to God. And it is on a high level. We don't have enough of that among believers today. We should all say, "Praise the Lord, and thanks be to God for His unspeakable gift." Can you say that from the heart? It is no good unless it comes from the heart. The filling of the Spirit produces a life of thankfulness so that we can honestly thank God for *all* things.

As I write this, there is a great deal of nonsense being promoted which I call sloppy agape. I heard recently, "Just say to everybody, 'I love you.'" My friend, if you don't love them, don't say it. If you do love them, *show* it.

Dr. Howard Kelly was a great surgeon and a great obstetrician. He wrote in the field of obstetrics, and his works were classic among doctors for a long time. He was also a great Christian, a wonderful man of God. The story is told of his taking a walk in the country outside the city of Baltimore in one of those lovely rural areas. He became thirsty and stopped at a farmhouse to ask for a drink of water. A little girl answered the door. She said that her parents had gone to town and there was no water in the house but there was cold milk down at the spring. Would he like a glass of milk? He said, "I surely would." So he sat on the porch while she got a glass of milk and brought it to him. My, it was delicious! She asked, "Would you like another glass?" He said, "I surely would." So she brought him another glass. He thanked her, then went on his way down the road, thinking what a lovely little girl she was. Not many days later the little girl became sick. She had a pain in her side and was taken to Johns Hopkins Hospital. Who do you suppose was the doctor who came in and examined her? It was Dr. Kelly, and he recognized her as the little girl who had given him the glasses of milk. He performed the necessary surgery and took special care of her. When it was time for her to go home, her parents came for her and waited anxiously for the bill because they didn't have the money to pay for the operation and the hospital costs. When the bill was presented to them, they opened it with trembling hands. Under the total balance was written, "Paid in full with two glasses of milk," signed "Dr. Howard Kelly." This was love in action, and the love he expressed was the fruit of the Spirit, because Dr. Kelly was a wonderful Christian.

My friend, you don't have to run around telling everyone you love them—*show* them that you love them. Be filled with the Spirit so there will be love and joy and thanksgiving in your life. This is very practical. This is down where the rubber meets the road.

Why don't you "drive into the filling station" and ask God to fill you up? The old gas tank is empty. You and I don't have anything worthwhile in ourselves. We need to go to Him and tell Him that we are empty and that we need the filling of the Holy Spirit so we can live for Him. We need to see that it is an impossibility by ourselves but that He can do it through us.

Let me repeat this because it is so important: we are told to be filled with the Holy Spirit—this is the only command given to the believer relative to the Holy Spirit. The other ministries of the Holy Spirit are accomplished in us when we receive Christ. Every believer is *regenerated* by the Holy Spirit. "But as many as received him, to them gave he power to become the sons of God . . ." (John 1:12). The believer is also *indwelt* by the Spirit.". . . Now if any man have not the Spirit of Christ, he is none of his" (Rom. 8:9). And the believer is *sealed* by the Holy Spirit ". . . in whom also after that ye believed, ye were sealed with that holy Spirit of promise" (Eph. 1:13). Also the believer is *baptized* by the Holy Spirit. "For by one Spirit are we all baptized into one body . . ." (1 Cor. 12:13). These four ministries of the Holy Spirit take place the moment the believer puts his trust in Christ. It is all accomplished for us. The only thing which is left up to us is to obey His command to be *filled* with the Holy Spirit (see v. 18).

Submitting yourselves one to another in the fear of God [Eph. 5:21].

"Submit" is a very interesting word. It does not mean obey. Paul is not saying that the child of God is a buck private in the rear rank taking orders from somebody in the church who thinks he is a sergeant or a captain. We do take orders, but they are from the Captain of our salvation.

Joshua thought he was a general of the children of Israel. He saw a Man with His sword drawn standing at the edge of the camp. He asked, ". . . Art thou for us, or for our adversaries?" If I may put it in good old Americana, he said, "Who told you to draw a sword? I'm the general here!" It was actually a rebuke. Then that One (who was the preincarnate Christ) turned and said, ". . . Nay; but as captain of the host of the Lord am I now come . . ." (Josh. 5:13–14). Joshua went down on his face and even took off his shoes because he was on holy ground. He learned that he had a Captain.

You and I are under a Captain, but the relationship is not military but on the basis of love. Our Lord said, "If ye love me, keep my commandments" (John 14:15). I think there is an alternative there: "If you don't love me, forget the commandments."

Now we see here that you and I are to submit ourselves "one to another in the fear of God." That doesn't mean we are to salute and fall down before some human being who outranks us. It does mean that in the fear of Christ we are to walk with one another in lowliness of mind.

If you will turn back to chapter 4, verses 1-2, you will see that Paul begins this section by saying that our walk should be in lowliness and meekness. That is the same thing that we have here. But notice in chapter 4 it begins with "I . . . beseech you." This is not a command. It is the language of love. The fires of Sinai have died down, and now it is based on what has been done by Christ at Calvary. It is based on the grace of God. "I therefore, the prisoner of the Lord, beseech you that ye walk worthy of the vocation wherewith ye are called, with all lowliness and meekness. . . ."

"Submitting yourselves one to another in the fear of God." This means that you do not try to run the church. Pastors, officers in the church, members of the church, all of us are to submit ourselves one to another in the fear of Christ. It cannot be a "my way" proposition. No one can say, "I want you to know that I'll do as I please. If I want to do it this way, I will do it this way." Such an attitude is not a mark of a Spirit-filled believer. Submitting ourselves one to another in the fear of God is another mark of being Spirit-filled.

> **Wives, submit yourselves unto your own husbands, as unto the Lord.**
>
> **For the husband is the head of the wife, even as Christ is the head of the church: and he is the saviour of the body.**
>
> **Therefore as the church is subject unto Christ, so let the wives be to their own husbands in every thing [Eph. 5:22-24].**

I have been doing some research on the word *submit*, and I have some rather startling things to tell you. The word *submit* relative to wives needs to be understood a little differently from the way it has been so often interpreted in the past. It is not, "Wives, *obey* your husbands."

Submit is a very mild word. It is a loving word. It means to respond to your own husband as unto the Lord. The way we respond to the Lord is that we love Him because He first loved us. And notice that it says "unto your own husbands." A very personal, loving relationship is the ground for submission. Paul is definitely speaking to believers about Christian marriage.

In this relationship of husband and wife, the man is the aggressor. He is the aggressor physically. He is the one who makes love. He is the aggressor in the home. He should be the breadwinner, the one who goes out with the lunch pail each day. And that doesn't give him the authority to be a top sergeant in the home either, by the way. The wife is to respond to him as the believer is to respond to Christ—in a love relationship.

A rough old boy came to my office one day with a request. He said, "Dr. McGee, I want you to talk to my wife. She's very cold, and she's not acting as a wife should." He didn't know it, but that was a dead giveaway—he was admitting failure as a husband. He showed what kind of a husband he was to draw that kind of response. I asked him, "Have you told her lately that you love her?" He said, "No. She knows I love her. I don't need to tell her that." I said to him, "I think you do. She does not need to tell you that she loves you until you say it first."

Woman is the responder, and man is the aggressor. The man is to say, "I love you," and he is the one who does the proposing. She is the one to say, "Yes." No woman is asked to say "I love you" to a man until he has said "I love you." When a man says he has a cold wife, it is because she has a cold husband. He is not being the husband that he should be. It is not her business to be the aggressor. Her role is the sweet submission of love.

"The husband is the head of the wife, even as Christ is the head of the church." In what way? It is a love relationship, and the husband is to be the head for the sake of order. You will find in this section of Ephesians that there are four different areas in which there is headship for the sake of order. Wives are to be subject to their husbands. Husbands are to be subject to Christ. Children are to be subject to parents. Servants are to be subject to masters. It is to be a sweet subjection, a willing subjection to someone who loves you. It is to be that kind of relationship. If there is no love in it, the idea of submission isn't worth a snap of the finger.

I have done a great deal of marriage counseling in my day, and I would say that 75 percent of the fault in marriages is on the side of the men. It is the man who is to keep the lovelight burning. In the beautiful Song of Solomon, the bridegroom says to the bride, "Behold, thou art fair, my love; behold, thou art fair . . ." (Song 1:15), and she responds, "My beloved is mine, and I am his . . ." (Song 2:16). He expresses his love first, and then she responds.

I know someone will say I am very idealistic and romantic about all this. Well, back in the Garden of Eden God made them that way. God started off with a romantic pair, Adam and Eve. Probably He didn't give that woman to Adam until Adam realized that he needed someone. She was given as a *helpmeet*. A helpmeet is just the other half of man. Man is half a man without a wife. God joined them together and called them Adam—not the Adams.

Some young man will say, "Preacher, I'm not that kind of person. I'm no hero." May I say to you that God never said that every girl would fall in love with you. Ninety-nine women may pass you by and see in you only the uninteresting boy next door. But one day there will come a woman who will see in you the knight in shining armor. It is God who gives that highly charged chemistry between a certain man and a certain woman.

My wife told me she thought I was the knight in shining armor. I want to tell you how it ended. Perhaps you have seen the television commerical of a knight in armor riding across the screen holding a can of cleanser. Do you know where he ended up? In that kitchen! Now that I am retired, that is where I have ended up. A friend of mine told me, "Now that you are retired, do things with your wife. When she washes tne dishes, you wash the dishes with her. When she mops the floor, you mop the floor with her!" Well, I'm not about to do that, but I surely do wash dishes more than I ever did before.

Now let me say a word to you if you are a young woman. Perhaps you are not beautiful of face or figure. God never said you would attract every male—only animals do that. Ninety-nine men will pass you by and see no more in you than what Kipling described as a rag, a bone, and a hank of hair. But one day there will come by a man who will love you if you are the right kind of person. You will become his inspiration. You may inspire him to greatness—perhaps to write a book or to compose a masterpiece. If you are his inspiration, do not ignore him, do not run from him. God may have put you together for that very purpose.

You may be saying, "Preacher, you're in the realm of theory. What you are talking about is idealistic. It sounds good in a storybook, but it doesn't happen in real life." You are wrong. It does happen.

Matthew Henry wrote the driest commentary I have ever read in my life, but, I want to tell you, he had a wonderful, romantic life as a young preacher. You would never think in reading his commentary that he was ever a romantic, but he was. In London he met a girl who belonged to the nobility. He was just a poor boy, but he fell in love with her and she loved him. Finally she went to her father to tell him about it, and her father tried to discourage her. He said, "That young man has no background. You don't even know where he came from." She answered, "You are right. I don't know where he came from, but I know where he is going, and I want to go with him!" And she did.

Nathaniel Hawthorne was a clerk. He worked in a government customs office in New York City, and he was fired for inefficiency. He came home and sat down discouraged and defeated. His wife came up and put her arm around him and said, "Now, Nathaniel, you can do what you always wanted to do: you can *write*." He wrote *The House of the Seven Gables, The Scarlet Letter*, "The Great Stone Face," and other great works. So, you see, it does work out in life. It has worked out in the lives of multitudes of folk.

Paul's instructions regarding the home teach that the Christian home is to be a mirror of the relation between Christ and the church. Christ's relationship to the church is different from the relationship of husband and wife in that "Christ is the head of the church: and he is the saviour of the body." The husband is not the savior of the wife. But in the realm of submission the wife should be subject to the husband and to the Lord Jesus Christ.

THE EXPECTATION OF THE CHURCH

Husbands, love your wives, even as Christ also loved the church, and gave himself for it [Eph. 5:25].

God never asked a woman to submit to any man who doesn't love her and love her like this. Oh, this is Christian love on a high plane. Today young people are finding out about sex, and there are innumerable books on the subject of marriage. I may sound to you like an antiquated preacher when I say that they are nonsense. Only the Christian can know what is real love in marriage, because it is carried to the high plane of the relationship between Christ and the church. There is nothing else like that, my friend.

That he might sanctify and cleanse it with the washing of water by the word [Eph. 5:26].

"Christ also loved the church, and gave himself for it"—that is in the *past*. In the *present* He is sanctifying the church with the water of the Word of God. The cleanser, which is the Bible, is better than any cleanser advertised on radio or television. The Word of God will not only take out the soiled spots, it will keep you from getting further spots in your life.

That he might present it to himself a glorious church, not having spot, or wrinkle, or any such thing; but that it should be holy and without blemish [Eph. 5:27].

In the *future* He will present it to Himself a glorious church, without a spot or wrinkle but holy and without blemish. We will see the church presented to Christ as a bride adorned for her husband when we study the Book of Revelation. May I say that every woman is beautiful on her wedding day. I have officiated at many weddings during my lifetime, and I have never seen an ugly bride. I have seen them before and after their wedding day, and I can't honestly say that all of them are beautiful. But on the day of their marriage they are beautiful.

No young man engaged to a young lady thinks that she ought to be put through the fires of persecution or the Great Tribulation before he marries her. That is unheard of. So imagine anyone saying that the church must go through the Great Tribulation! She is engaged to *Him*, and He is cleansing the church by the washing of the Word of God. Keep in mind that when we use the word *church* we are not talking about an organization with a steeple, a pulpit, and an organ. We are talking about the body of true believers. This verse means that He is washing each believer, preparing each one for that great event. I believe that is something which is really taking place in our day.

So we have seen the past, present, and future. Christ loved the church and gave Himself for it. He is sanctifying the church with the washing of water by the Word. In the future the church will be presented to Him as a radiant bride with all sin removed. Then the church will be holy and unblamable.

So ought men to love their wives as their own bodies. He that loveth his wife loveth himself.

For no man ever yet hated his own flesh; but nourisheth and cherisheth it, even as the Lord the church:

For we are members of his body, of his flesh, and of his bones.

For this cause shall a man leave his father and mother, and shall be joined unto his wife, and they two shall be one flesh.

This is a great mystery: but I speak concerning Christ and the church [Eph. 5:28–32].

I have quoted this entire passage so you can see how Paul draws on these two themes and goes back and forth, husband and wife, Christ and the church. After talking about Christ and the church, the subject goes back to husband and wife: "So ought men to love their wives as their own bodies."

The thing a couple needs for their marriage ceremony is not a champagne supper. They both need to be filled with the Holy Spirit. They will have the greatest honeymoon that any couple ever had. Those sophisticated boys and girls who talk about sex and extramarital relationships today don't even know what real love is. They know a lot about sex, but they do not know anything at all about the beauty and the ecstasy and the sweetness of a real Christian marriage.

The husband is to love his wife because the marriage relationship makes the wife a part of his own body. It is like the church is the body of Christ and Christ is the head of that body. On this basis the husband is the head of the wife. It is unnatural for a man to hate his own flesh, so the husband is to love his wife because she is his own flesh.

Christ, knowing the weakness of the church, nourishes and cherishes her. Husbands are to do the same.

Verse 31 is a quotation from Genesis 2:24. Paul here refers to the relationship that existed in the Garden of Eden between Adam and Eve. That first couple is a figure of the future union of Christ and the church as Bridegroom and bride. Eve was created to be a helpmeet for Adam. She was taken from his side, not molded from the ground as were the animals. Adam was incomplete until they were together. God fashioned her, and I think she was the loveliest thing in creation when God brought her to Adam. One wag has said that she had to be better looking than man because God had practiced on man but He had experience when He made woman. She was a helpmeet for Adam. She compensated for what he lacked. She was made for him and they became one. In the Hebrew the word for "man" is *ish* and for "woman" it is *isha*. The word is almost the same—she was taken out of man.

I have two illustrations, taken from history, of this wonderful relationship between man and woman. That kind of thing is often lost today. The "new" morality and sexual freedom are putting a lot of young people in slavery. It simply will not work. God meant for Christians to have this relationship on a much higher plane.

The first illustration is the story of Abelard and Heloïse. When John Lord wrote his *Great Women,* he used Heloïse as the example of love, marital love. The story concerns a young ecclesiastic by the name of Abelard. He was a brilliant young teacher and preacher in what became the University of Paris. The canon had a niece by the name of Heloïse whom he sent to be under Abelard's instruction. She was a remarkable person; he was a remarkable man. You know the story—they fell madly in love. But according to the awful practice of that day the marriage of a priest was deemed a lasting disgrace. When John Lord wrote their story, he gave this introduction which I would like to share with you. It is almost too beautiful to read in this day. It is like a dew-drenched breeze blowing from a flower-strewn mountain meadow over the slop bucket and pigsty of our contemporary literature. Here is what he wrote:

> When Adam and Eve were expelled from Paradise, they yet found one flower, wherever they wandered, blooming in perpetual beauty. This flower represents a great certitude, without which few would be happy,—subtle, mysterious, inexplicable,—a great boon recognized alike by poets and moralists, Pagan and Christian; yea, identified not only with happiness, but human existence, and pertaining to the soul in its highest aspirations. Allied with the transient and the mortal, even with the weak and corrupt, it is yet immortal in its nature and lofty in its aims,—at once a passion, a sentiment, and an inspiration.
>
> To attempt to describe woman without this element of our complex nature, which constitutes her peculiar fascination, is like trying to act the tragedy of Hamlet without Hamlet himself,—an absurdity; a picture without a central figure, a novel without a heroine, a religion without a sacrifice. My subject is not without its difficulties. The passion or sentiment is degrading when perverted, it is exalting when pure. Yet it is not vice I would paint, but virtue; not weakness, but strength; not the transient, but the permanent; not the mortal, but the immortal,—all that is ennobling in the aspiring soul.

Abelard and Heloïse, having fallen in love, were not permitted by the church to marry. Therefore they were married secretly by a friend of Abelard. He continued to teach. But the secret came out when a servant betrayed them, and she was forced into a nunnery. Abelard was probably the boldest thinker whom the Middle Ages produced. At the beginning of the twelfth century he began to preach and teach that the Word of God was man's authority, not the church. This man, a great man, became bitter and sarcastic in his teaching because of what had been denied him. When he was on his deathbed, for he died a great while before Heloïse, being twenty years her senior, he asked that she be permitted to come to see him. The church did the cruelest thing of all—they would not allow her to come. Therefore he penned her a letter. To me it is the most pathetic thing I have ever read. He concludes it with this prayer: "When it pleased Thee, O Lord, and as it pleased Thee, Thou didst join us, and Thou didst separate us. Now, what Thou hast so mercifully begun, mercifully complete; and after separating us in this world, join us together eternally in heaven." And I believe in God's heaven they are together.

John Wesley's story is not told in England; it is told in this country, in Georgia. When John Wesley came as a young missionary to Georgia, the crown had already sent a nobleman out there—I think they wanted to get rid of him at court because he was an insipid fellow, devoid of personality and masculinity. Yet due to the terrible custom of that day, the nobility was entitled to marry the finest, and he had married a woman not only of striking beauty and strong personality, but one who was an outstanding Christian. Then there came into their colony this fiery young missionary. Again you know the story—they fell in love. And that happens to be John Wesley's love story. He begged her to flee with him and go live among the Indians. She said, "No, John, God has called you to go back to England, and He has called you to do some great service for Him." It was she who sent John Wesley back to England. The night came for his ship to sail; they had to wait for the tide and the wind, and she came down to bid him good-bye. Oh, yes, she held him that night and he held her, but even the worst critics of Wesley say that nothing took place that was wrong. He still begged her to go with him among the Indians and live. The biographer of Wesley says that he came down that gangplank twice, but she sent him back, back to England—to marry the Methodist church. He returned to England a brokenhearted man; yet she had become his inspiration.

It is God who gives this kind of love to believers who are filled with the Holy Spirit. May I say to the young people today: Don't accept anything that is second-rate. Don't take anything but the very best that God has to offer you.

Nevertheless let every one of you in particular so love his wife even as himself; and the wife see that she reverence her husband [Eph. 5:33].

"Nevertheless" brings us down to earth with a jolt. This is the practical part about marriage. Oh, how sin has marred this glorious relationship—as it has marred everything else—but this relationship can be yours if you want it to be the best.

Paul brings the reader back to the ordinary routine of Christian living in the home. "Let each love his wife as himself." This shows the kind of husband to whom the wife is to be in subjection. The husband and the wife in the home are to set forth in simplicity the mystery of the coming glory. This is a very practical application of that which is highly idealistic. He brings the romantic into the realm of reality.

CHAPTER 6

THEME: The church is a soldier; the soldier's relation-ships; the soldier's enemy; the soldier's protection; the soldier's example—Paul was a good soldier of Christ; benediction

In the preceding chapter the church was designated as the *bride* of Christ. Now in this chapter it is to be a good soldier of Jesus Christ. I have told you that my humorous friend says this sequence is to be expected—after a couple gets married, the war begins. Therefore, the church should be a good soldier. He was being facetious, of course. In the *future* the church is to be presented as the bride of Christ. This is the expectation of the church. Today is the period of the engagement and exhibition of the church before the world.

Now the chapter before us presents another side of the life of a believer. In the world today the church is to be a good soldier of Jesus Christ. In Ephesus there stood the great temple of Diana, one of the seven wonders of the ancient world. It stood for all that was pagan and heathen; it was grossly immoral. It was time for the believers in Ephesus to recognize that they had an enemy. Not only did the Christians in Ephesus have an enemy, but we have an enemy today. Our enemy is not the worship at the temple of Diana. I think we have something infinitely worse than that. We are seeing immorality and heathenism not only in the name of religion but actually in the name of *Christianity*—when it is not Christian at all!

The first part of the chapter opens with instructions to children, parents, servants, and masters. This may seem foreign to the life of a soldier. However, a soldier's training does not start in boot camp; it begins when he is a child in the home.

In World War II they had a saying in the navy that in the early days of our nation we had wooden ships and iron men, but now we have iron ships and paper-doll men. That is probably not entirely accurate, but a report from the Great Lakes Naval Training Station tells us that a shocking percentage of all young men in the United States attaining the age of navy enlistment years must be rejected because of previous criminal records and because of personality, psychological, or health problems; also an alarming number of all enlistees fail to measure up to recruit training. Severe problems are faced in the training of young men who must be trained in the simple things that should have been learned at home. At seventeen a young man ought to be ready to launch into the training program. The navy finds that they can easily put a uniform on the man. It is putting a man into the uniform that is causing such problems.

This same type of breakdown is attested to by foreign mission boards. A survey reveals that a very small percentage of students graduating from Christian Bible schools and colleges go into foreign missions, and a startling number return after the first term as casualities. Training is essential if the soldier is to fight properly and be victorious over the enemy.

The preparation of a soldier must begin in the home when he is a child—not in the church or in the Sunday school but in the home. Every child who doesn't get that first lesson is handicapped. One of the great problems of our young people today, and some older ones too, is that they were not properly trained in the home. Proper training means discipline.

THE SOLDIER'S RELATIONSHIPS

Children, obey your parents in the Lord: for this is right [Eph. 6:1].

It is right because it is according to the will of God. It is actually more than right; it is just. It is a righteous thing to do because it is God's way.

The first lesson that a soldier must learn is obedience to those in authority. He must follow orders. This basic training is learned in the home. After the soldier has learned to obey, then he is in a position to be promoted to the rank of an officer where he gives commands to others. To know how to give orders depends largely on how the soldier learned to obey. This basic training is found in the home with the parent-child relationship, and then with the master-servant relationship. The victories of the Christian life are won in the home and in the place of business.

You will remember that it is said of the Lord Jesus that as a boy He went down to Nazareth, and He was subject to Joseph and Mary.

There are two essential factors which must be taken into account in this verse and in this section:

1. It is assumed that Paul is talking about a Christian home, a home such as he had been discussing in chapter 5 regarding the marriage relationship. Obedience of children to parents is confined to the circumference of "in the Lord." Christian parents have the privilege of claiming their children for the Lord. I think we all should do that. Even where only one parent is a believer, he may claim his children for God. "For the unbelieving husband is sanctified by the wife, and the unbelieving wife is sanctified by the husband: else were your children unclean; but now are they holy" (1 Cor. 7:14). This, of course, does not mean that the child is a believer just because he has a Christian parent. It does mean that the parent has a right to claim that child.

Notice that it says, "Obey your parents in the Lord." I have great sympathy for a boy who accepts the Lord and has an unsaved father or mother. There may be times when such a child must obey God rather than men.

2. The word for "obey" here is different from the word found in verse 22 of chapter 5. The wife is to submit. The wife occupies a place of equality with the husband, and submission is merely a question of headship. Here the child is to obey as the servant is to obey—the same word is used in verse 5.

Disobedience to parents is the last and lowest form of lawlessness to occur on this earth. "This know also, that in the last days perilous times shall come. For men shall be lovers of their own selves, covetous, boasters, proud, blasphemers, disobedient to parents, unthankful, unholy" (2 Tim. 3:1–2). Disobedience to parents is one of the characteristics of the last days. Today we hear of many cases of children rejecting parental authority and even killing their parents! This is indicative of the times in which we live.

Of course there will come a time in a boy's life when he begins to rebel against his parents because it is time for him to move out and get married and start a home of his own. God has given him a nature that rebels against being a mama's boy, tied to his mama's apron strings for the rest of his life. God wants him to stand on his own two feet. This kind of rebellion, this struggle for independence, is different from disobedience.

When I was a pastor, I remember visiting in a home in which the father and I couldn't even carry on a conversation because his little boy occupied the center ring of the circus. He was a little circus himself, and if you ask me, the dear little fellow was a brat. The father said, "I just can't make that child obey me." The father weighed about two hundred pounds, and the boy weighed about thirty pounds. Yet the father said, "I just can't make him obey me." Well, I think he *could* have, and I think he *should* have. God intended for the father to make him obey at that age.

Honour thy father and mother; which is the first commandment with promise;

That it may be well with thee, and thou mayest live long on the earth [Eph. 6:2–3].

We have learned that the Ten Commandments are not the norm for Christian living—but that doesn't mean you can *break* them. A youngster in the home is to honor father and mother, and as we grow older we are to continue to honor them by the life that we live. (It is interesting that all the Ten Commandments are repeated in the New Testament with the exception of the commandment concerning the Sabbath day.) Honoring your father and mother carries with it a promise of long life to those who keep it (see Exod. 20:12), and that promise is repeated here. It is the first commandment with promise. The other commandments promised something if they were *not* kept, but they didn't promise anything if they were kept.

Samson and Absalom are two examples in Scripture of boys who did not follow this commandment, and their lives were short. Samson, a judge, died when he was a young man. Absalom rebelled against his father David, and he was killed when he was a young man.

And, ye fathers, provoke not your children to wrath: but bring them up in the nurture and admonition of the Lord [Eph. 6:4].

"Nurture" means discipline, and "admonition" means instruction. Bring them up in the discipline and instruction of the Lord. No such commandment was given to parents under the Law. Under grace there are always mutual responsibilities and interactive duties. The parent is not to vent a bad disposition on a child or punish him in a fit of rage. It is the parents' duty to teach the child the truths of the Scriptures and then to live them before the child. Don't provoke your children to wrath. As a believer, you are to live at home like a believer.

"Fathers" includes the mothers also. However, the emphasis, I think, is on the father because the disciplining and training of the child is actually his responsibility, but it does include the mother also.

Children are not to be provoked to anger. This doesn't mean that they are to be treated as if they were a cross between an orchid and a piece of Dresden china. I think that the board of education should be applied to the seat of learning whenever it is needed. The writer of Proverbs had a great deal to say about this: "He that spareth his rod hateth his son: but he that loveth him chasteneth him betimes" (Prov. 13:24). "Chasten thy son while there is hope, and let not thy soul spare for his crying" (Prov. 19:18). "Foolishness is bound in the heart of a child; but the rod of correction shall drive it far from him" (Prov. 22:15). "Withhold not correction from the child: for if thou beatest him with the rod, he shall not die. Thou shalt beat him with the rod and shalt deliver his soul from hell" (Prov. 23:13–14). "The rod and reproof give wisdom: but a child left to himself bringeth his mother to shame. . . . Correct thy son, and he shall give thee rest; yea, he shall give delight unto thy soul" (Prov. 29:15, 17).

There is the story of the father whipping the little boy and saying, "Son, this hurts me more than it hurts you." The boy replied, "Yeah, but not in the same place!"

These little ones who simply will not obey need to be spanked. They need a trip to the woodshed. A child should never be whipped while the parent is angry; this is stated very clearly. We are never to provoke our children to wrath, which will happen if they see that we are simply venting a mean disposition on them. They should be disciplined.

In Proverbs 23 we are told that when we spank our children they won't die. I can remember that my mother whipped me a great deal more than my father did. She was the one at home with us, so she would get a switch and she could make it hurt. I was such a good boy I don't know why it was that I got such a number of switchings! I did learn that if I would yell at the top of my voice, "You're killing me, you're killing me," she would always let up because she didn't want the neighbors to hear and say, "My, that poor boy's mother is killing him!" I found out it sort of softened the punishment. Of course, she wasn't trying to kill me. She was giving me the punishment I needed.

"Correct thy son, and he shall give thee rest . . . [and] delight unto thy soul"—a child in a Christian home should be given Christian instruction so that he might come to a vital relationship with Christ and be fortified when he comes in contact with the world. Every parent ought to have the privilege of leading his child to a saving knowledge of Christ.

My wife was never my assistant pastor—I insisted on that. I never let her become president of the missionary society or hold any office in any women's organization in any church that I served. When I accepted a pastorate, I told my board. "My wife is my *wife*. She is not the assistant pastor. Her business is to take care of the home and the child." I think that is important. My wife had the privilege that I'm afraid very few parents have today. I was out on a trip and my wife was visiting with her mother. Our daughter was about seven or eight years old at the time. She came in and said, "Mama, I want to accept Jesus." My wife took her into the bedroom and got down on her knees with her and had the privilege of leading her own little girl to the Lord. I always felt that this was much more important than to try to be a personal worker in the church. I know a great number of personal workers in the church who have lost their own children. My friend, your first responsibility is to your own child. You had better concentrate on that child—do that instead of tending to everyone else's business and trying to raise everyone else's children. I realize it won't make me popular to make such a statement, but God's Word makes it clear that He gives us the responsibility for our own children.

"Bring them up in the nurture [discipline] . . . of the Lord." Notice again that the discipline is to be *of the Lord.* The discipline and instruction are to be administered in the name of the Lord. That is important. Paul has taken the subject of submission first into the home with the husband and wife relationship, then with the parent-child relationship. Now he moves out of the home into the street, the workshop, the marts of trade. It is a different situation here, for there are no bonds of love such as are found in a home; yet children of God who are filled with the Holy Spirit will be submissive one to another.

> **Servants, be obedient to them that are your masters according to the flesh, with fear and trembling, in singleness of your heart, as unto Christ;**
>
> **Not with eye-service, as men-pleasers; but as the servants of Christ, doing the will of God from the heart;**
>
> **With good will doing service, as to the Lord, and not to men:**
>
> **Knowing that whatsoever good thing any man doeth, the same shall he receive of the Lord, whether he be bond or free [Eph. 6:5-8].**

Servants (lit., slaves) are to be obedient to masters according to the flesh, meaning the masters down here on earth. Servants are not to serve with eyeservice—with one eye on the clock or working only when the boss is looking. They are not to serve as "men-pleasers." In other words, they are not to butter up the boss. Service is to be done as the servants of Christ, doing the will of God from the soul.

There is a responsibility put upon a believer who is a laborer and also a responsibility put upon one who is a capitalist or an employer. This is the employer-employee relationship. In Paul's day it was an even sharper division than it is now—it was really master and slave. Remember that this entire section began in chapter 5, verse 21, which says, "Submitting yourselves one to another in the fear of God." That sounds all right for Sunday, for the church service, but what about Monday morning when we go to work? Christian workers working for Christian owners of the factory will not need a labor boss to go to the capitalist and tell him what to do. I know of several businesses run by dedicated Christians. They have chapel service on company time, and they pay their workers while they are attending chapel. They are prosperous—God has blessed them. They don't need a union. An employee in one of these companies told me, "If we were under a union, we wouldn't be making what we are making right here." We are talking about Christians, Christian workers and Christian owners. There are both sides to the coin. This gets right down to the nitty-gritty.

It is estimated that half of the 120 millions of people living in the Roman Empire were slaves. Christianity never attacked the evil of slavery. Rather it reached down to the slave in his degradation and lifted him up, assuring him of his liberty in Christ. The very nature of the gospel condemned slavery. It eventually broke the shackles of slavery from the bodies of men and cut the fetters from their minds and souls. Multitudes of slaves came to Christ, as we learn in Romans 16—many of those named there were slaves or members of the Praetorian guard.

In the United States of America the South had to lose the Civil War. I am a southerner, but I recognize the South had to lose because slavery was *wrong*. That doesn't mean that the North was right in the method used, but it does mean that the principle of slavery was wrong.

"Servants, be obedient to them that are your masters." Notice the Word of God says to "be *obedient*." This reveals that Christianity did not instigate revolution against the evil practice of slavery. It preached a gospel which was more revolutionary than revolution has ever been. Revolution has always had bad side effects, leaving bitterness and hatred which has lasted through the centuries. The gospel of Christ will break down the middle wall of partition—which in our day is prejudice and discrimination of one race against another—and will replace it with real brotherly love.

If the Word of God were preached as it was in the early days of these United States, and if those who profess to be Christian were obedient and loyal to those to whom they owe obedience and loyalty, it would change the entire complexion of American life today. A man is not a Christian just because he has made a profession of Christianity and calls himself a child of God on Sunday. Whether or not he is a genuine Christian is revealed by his loyalty to his employer, to his family, to his home, to his church, and to his pastor. When a professing Christian is disloyal in these areas of his life, the chances are he will also be disloyal to Christ. He certainly has no effective witness for Christ.

"Servants, be obedient to . . . your masters according to the flesh" makes it clear that slavery applied only to the bodies of men and not to their souls. This obedience was to be with "fear and trembling." This does not mean abject and base cringing before a master, but it does mean treating him with respect and dignity.

"In singleness of your heart" means there should not be any taint of duplicity. There should be no two-facedness. There should not be the licking of the boots of the employer when he is around and then stabbing him in the back when he is away. Such action should never be in the life of a Christian.

The servant's obedience is to be done "as unto Christ." This shows that the slave has been lifted from the base position of degradation where he sullenly worked as little as possible and only when his master was watching. Now he is the slave of Christ, and Christ has made him free. He is to look above the earthly master in his attempt to please his Master in heaven. An earthly master could control only the bodies of the slaves. The slaves of Christ have yielded their souls to Him, even their total personalities. Remember that Paul called himself the bondslave of Jesus Christ.

"With good will doing service" shows that their attitudes should reflect their Christian service. When a child of God—whether a slave or a master, employer or employee—gets to the place where the motive of his life is to please Christ, then the hurdles posed by capital and labor are easily passed over.

In our day there is a new kind of slavery, and it is sweeping over the nations of the world. In our own land there is a slavery that is not only of the body but of the mind. Such slavery is far more pernicious and deadly than that of the Roman Empire. Multiplied thousands are willing to make any sacrifice today to foreign ideology, and you can call it any name you choose.

I had the privilege of speaking to a group of university students from Berkeley, California. These young men, who are majoring in political economy, have turned to the Lord. There was a time when they were slaves to a particular system of political economy, but now they are delivered from that. One young man told me, "One time I thought we could manipulate the economy and that we could make everyone prosperous and happy. I see now that only Christ will be able to bring in that kind of a society. That doesn't mean we are not going to work for it, but it does mean that we know our goal is limited and only Christ can do it."

What can break a man's shackles? Only the power of the gospel of Christ. He will make you free. "If the Son therefore, shall make you free, ye shall be free indeed" (John 8:36). It is Christ who offers freedom. Think of the thousands today who are trapped by drugs and by alcohol. There is slavery on every side of us.

We should be slaves to Christ and to no one or nothing else. Saul of Tarsus was a slave to an ideology. He was a Pharisee. When he came to Christ, he was made free. However, immediately he yielded to a new Master and said, ". . . Lord, what wilt thou have me to do? . . ." (Acts 9:6). He had become a bondslave to Jesus Christ.

The Lord has lifted the employee to a high position; He has dignified labor. It doesn't make any difference whether a man is working at a bench or digging a ditch or working in an office or mining down in the bowels of the earth or farming the land on the top of the earth. If he is a child of God, he can say, "I serve the Lord Christ."

William Carey was a shoemaker who applied to go as a foreign missionary. Someone asked him, "What is your business?" meaning to humiliate him, because he was not an ordained minister. Carey answered, "My business is serving the Lord, and I make shoes to pay expenses." He was a servant of Christ. Oh, that men were that kind of worker today—it would change the whole labor scene.

> **And, ye masters, do the same things unto them, forbearing threatening: knowing that your Master also is in heaven; neither is there respect of persons with him [Eph. 6:9].**

Something is also said to the masters. If you are an employer, before Christ you are just another man. God is no respecter of persons. What He has said to labor also applies to you. You come under the same category since you also have a Master, and your Master is Christ. This is the Christian relationship of capital and labor. The responsibilities are mutual. Masters are not to take advantage of their position as master. They are not to abuse their power. They are not to threaten. In the presence of Christ, the master and the servant stand on the same footing. They are brothers in Christ.

We find a very practical demonstration of this in the Epistle to Philemon. Philemon was a master who had a slave named Onesimus. Onesimus ran away from his master, and according to the law of that day, his master could have put him to death. However, after Onesimus trusted Christ, Paul sent him back to his master with the letter to Philemon. This is what Paul wrote: "For perhaps he therefore departed for a season, that thou shouldest receive him for ever; not now as a servant, but above a servant, a brother beloved, specially to me, but how much more unto thee, both in the flesh, and in the Lord?" (Philem. 15–16). When both capital and labor are believers, they are brothers.

Don't tell me Christianity is not practical. It *is* practical, and it will work. A great Chinese Christian, who had attended college here in the United States and knew America pretty well, said, "It is not that in America Christianity has been tried and found wanting. The problem over there is it never has been tried." That is still the problem today—we have kept it behind stained glass windows. My friend, if Christianity cannot move out of the sanctuary and get down into the secular, there is something radically wrong. It will *work* if it is tried. It will work in this capital-labor relationship.

THE SOLDIER'S ENEMY

Now we come to the theme of this chapter, which is "the church is a good soldier of Jesus Christ." We have seen the Christian in his relationships: God begins with him in the home. Then God has something to say to him as he moves out into the world where he is either an employee or an employer—he has to be one or the other, and as a child of God he has to contribute to the welfare of contemporary society. He needs to be a producer one way or the other.

Now we learn of the soldier's enemy. There is a battle to be fought. One of the things that is commonly misunderstood today is that the child of God is in a battle, and the battle is being fought along *spiritual* lines.

If the duties which relate to the commonplace are not faithfully followed, there can be no great spiritual victories in the high realm of Christian attainments. It is pretty well known that I represent the fundamental position. I am premillennial, pretribulational, and a dispensationalist in my belief. I get a little weary and a little bored with folk who so insistently hold these same views, yet whose lives are lived in a very careless manner, not commensurate with this exalted, high position that we have. We are seated in the heavenlies! How wonderful. My friend, we are walking right down here on this earth, and our theology has to walk in shoeleather. If you are not living a life that pleases Christ, you are wasting your time attending Keswick conferences and Bible classes. Often in Christian circles we see a display of bitterness, vitriol, and hatred, which hurts the cause of Christ a great deal. Why is it that we can have so much exalted teaching and such low living? There are too many who are fundamental in their heads but liberal in their feet. There is a great danger in thinking that all we need is a head knowledge and a vocabulary so that we can spout out our position lucidly and fluently but can lead careless Christian lives. To do this is to misunderstand where the battle is being fought.

I do not think the devil is concentrating in the nightclubs or on skid row or in the underworld or in the Mafia. I think he is concentrating on the church on Sunday morning. He is working on the spiritual front, and too many sleepy Christians seem to be totally unaware of that. Too many Christians are concerned about closing up the cocktail parlors when they need to be closing their mouths from gossiping and criticizing. The devil is working in an area where we least expect to find him. He is not out on the town on Saturday night. He has gone to bed early so he can get up and go to church on Sunday morning. The spiritual battle is being fought wherever a man is giving out the Word of God, where a church is standing for the Word of God. That is the place the devil wants to destroy, and that is the place of the spiritual battle.

Sometimes the most dangerous place you can be is in church on Sunday morning. Where was the most dangerous place in Jerusalem the night Jesus was arrested? Was it with the Pharisees? Was it with the cutthroats of the underworld? No. The most dangerous place was in the Upper Room with Jesus. Do you know why? That is where the devil was that night. It is said that he entered into Judas Iscariot to betray Him. The devil was there. I believe both Judas Iscariot and Simon Peter would testify to the fact that that was the most dangerous place to have been that night in Jerusalem. We need to recognize where the battle is being fought.

You may remember that at the beginning of our study in this Epistle to the Ephesians I compared it to the Book of Joshua. What Joshua is to the Old Testament, Ephesians is to the New Testament. Joshua led the children of Israel across the Jordan River into the land of Canaan, and there were enemies in the land. There were battles to be fought, and there were victories to be won.

The Jordan River is not a picture of our death, and the Promised Land is not a picture of heaven. If you want to sing "On Jordan's stormy banks I stand and cast a wistful eye," you may, but that does not speak of our death. It actually speaks of the death and resurrection of Jesus Christ, and you and I cross over—through the death and resurrection of Christ—out of the wilderness of this world into Canaan. The child of God should be living today in Canaan. Remember that

Canaan does not represent heaven—it could not because there were enemies in Canaan and battles to be fought. You and I as believers are in the place of soldier service. The soldier's enemy is identified, and the battle is before us.

When Joshua entered the Promised Land, there were three enemies that confronted him. First there was the city of Jericho, standing right in the way. Jericho represents the world today. What Jericho was to Joshua, the world is to the Christian. Joshua was told to march around the city—not fight it. We cannot overcome the world by fighting the world. It is a mistake if we try that method. "For whatsoever is born of God overcometh the world: and this is the victory that overcometh the world, even our faith. Who is he that overcometh the world, but he that believeth that Jesus is the Son of God?" (1 John 5:4–5). The only way we can overcome the world is by our faith and trust in God. "Love not the world, neither the things that are in the world. If any man love the world, the love of the Father is not in him" (1 John 2:15). The things of the world are passing away, and the child of God is not to love them. Our experience here is to be a Canaan experience.

The second enemy confronted by Joshua was the little town of Ai. Ai represents the flesh. Joshua thought it would be easy to overcome Ai, so he sent up a small detachment, and they were really whipped. When they came back, Joshua got down on his face and began to whimper and cry before God. God told him, ". . . Get thee up; wherefore liest thou thus upon thy face? Israel hath sinned . . ." (Josh. 7:10–11). And that sin had to be confessed and put away before God would give Israel the victory. And this is what you and I must do if we are to overcome the flesh.

Many Christians have a victory over the world; they are marching around Jericho, tooting a horn as the children of Israel blew their trumpets, saying, "I don't do this and I don't do that." But they are being defeated by the flesh. They are overcome by temper. They are overcome by gossiping. One Christian man came to me and said, "Why in the world is it that I just continue to lie about everything?" Well, that's what the flesh will do. The flesh is getting the victory over many of us, my friend. Ai represents the flesh.

Then thirdly, Joshua had to contend with the Gibeonites. They were clever, sly rascals. They lived just over the hill, but they took old, moldy bread and wore worn-out shoes and made everything look as if they had come on a long journey. They came into the camp where Joshua was and said, "Brother, we have heard about you. My, we've heard how God delivered you from Egypt and gave you victories over Sihon and Og, and we want to make a treaty with you. We want to be your friends" (see Josh. 9:4–11). That is the way the devil approaches us. He is the deceiver, and he makes his ministers seem like angels of light.

Someone described a leader of a cult by saying, "I listen to that man. He is so attractive, so personable. He is really wonderful, and what he says thrills me." Now listen to this and remember it: ". . . for Satan himself is transformed into an angel of light. Therefore it is no great thing if his ministers also be transformed as the ministers of righteousness; whose end shall be according to their works" (2 Cor. 11:14–15). Do you think that the devil is going to knock at your door and say, "Look, I'm the devil; I'm here to take you in; I'm here to fool you"? Obviously, that is not the way the devil will approach you. He will use every possible way to deceive you. He may send someone to knock at your door and offer you literature that will "explain" the Bible. Or, he may approach you this way if you are in a church that is going liberal: "Remember, grandpa had a pew in the church and that window over there is named for grandma. You can't afford to leave this church because you have so much invested here." The Word of God says, "Wherefore come out from among them, and be ye separate, saith the Lord . . ." (2 Cor. 6:17). And the devil says, "But we really need you here, so why don't you just stick around?" You see, he is subtle.

The Gibeonites represent the devil. They fooled Joshua, and he made a treaty with them. They were the ones who got him into trouble. At Ai the sin had to be confessed and dealt with severely before God would give them the victory, and that is the way we overcome the flesh. But what about the Gibeonites? Joshua made an alliance with them, and they gave him trouble. If we line up with Satan, we will find ourselves defeated. What can we do? Listen: We *cannot* overcome him ourselves. You and I are no match for the devil. We are not even told to fight the devil. We are told that God will fight for us.

Finally, my brethren, be strong in the Lord, and in the power of his might [Eph. 6:10].

Allow me to again use my translation: "Finally (in conclusion) be strengthened in the Lord, and in the power of His might. Put on the armor *(panoplian)* of God in order that ye may be able to stand against the strategems *(methodias)* of the devil. For our wrestling is not against blood and flesh, but against the principalities, against powers, against the world rulers of this darkness, against the spiritual hosts of evil in the heavenly (places and things)."

Put on the whole armour of God, that ye may be able to stand against the wiles of the devil [Eph. 6:11].

What in the world is Paul talking about? He is talking about spiritual wickedness, about that which is satanic. Notice that he is coming to the end of the epistle and says, "In conclusion be strengthened in the Lord, and in the power of His might." You cannot overcome the devil in your own strength and your own power. Paul is definitely making a play upon two Greek words: The *panoplian* of God is needed and available to meet the *methodias* of the devil. "Be strengthened in the Lord"—that is the only place you and I get power.

For we wrestle not against flesh and blood, but against principalities, against powers, against the rulers of the darkness of this world, against spiritual wickedness in high places [Eph. 6:12].

The enemy whom the Christian is to fight is *not* flesh and blood. The enemy is spiritual, and the warfare is spiritual. That is why we need spiritual power. It is well to note that the flesh of the believer is not the enemy to be fought. The believer is to reckon the flesh dead and to *yield* to God. The way of victory over the flesh is outlined in Romans

6. Fighting the old nature will lead to defeat, and Paul records such an experience in Romans 7.

It is only God's armor which can withstand the strategy and onslaught of Satan who has all kinds of weapons (spiritual missiles). We need an antimissile system if we are going to overcome him. That is why it is so important for the Christian soldier to recognize that he does not fight an enemy who is flesh and blood. We are not to fight other men. The enemy is spiritual, and the warfare is spiritual. The devil is the enemy of every believer and the one here whom we are told we fight. The way to victory over the devil is to obey the commands to "put on the whole armour of God" and "to stand" (v. 11).

We are in a spiritual battle. The devil has in battle array his minions arranged by ranks. It says that we wrestle against them. This speaks of the hand-to-hand encounter with the spiritual forces of wickedness. The translation of verse twelve is not as strong as it should be. It should actually read, "For our wrestling is not against blood and flesh, but against the principalities, against powers, against the world rulers of this darkness [and these are all spiritual], against the spiritual hosts of evil in the heavenly places." This is our warfare, and it's in progress now.

There is a demonic world around us and it is manifesting itself at the present hour. If I had said this when I was a young preacher, many would not have believed it. Or they would have said as did one dear lady, "Dr. McGee, you sound positively spooky." Today, however, demonism is a popular subject and is plainly exhibited. We have the Church of Satan in many of our cities. There are strange things happening to certain of these weird, way-out groups. A man said to me recently, "Dr. McGee, this thing is real today." Who said it wasn't real? If you are an unbeliever in this area, open your eyes and see what is happening about us. People are being ensnared and led into all kinds of demonism. There are spiritual forces working in the world, evil forces working against the church. They are working against the believer, against God, against Christ. Don't try to pooh pooh these things. It is happening, and you and I alone are no match for it.

The fact that there is a spiritual enemy to overcome is well illustrated in the tenth chapter of the Book of Daniel. Daniel had been praying, and he didn't get any answer. He had been praying for three weeks. "In those days I Daniel was mourning three full weeks. I ate no pleasant bread, neither came flesh nor wine in my mouth, neither did I anoint myself at all, till three whole weeks were fulfilled" (Dan. 10:2–3). Finally, an angel came and touched him and said, ". . . O Daniel, a man greatly beloved, understand the words that I speak unto thee, and stand upright: for unto thee am I now sent. And when he had spoken this word unto me, I stood trembling. Then said he unto me, Fear not, Daniel: for from the first day that thou didst set thine heart to understand, and to chasten thyself before thy God, thy words were heard, and I am come for thy words" (Dan. 10:11–12). If that was true, then Daniel had every right to ask, "Then where in the world have you been for three weeks?" Listen to the angel continue, "But the prince of the kingdom of Persia withstood me one and twenty days: but, lo, Michael, one of the chief princes, came to help me; and I remained there with the kings of Persia" (Dan. 10:13). He was in conflict with a demon, and he had to go back for reinforcement. This was a spiritual battle that was going on, and we likewise have one today.

We have said that these powers are organized. *Principalities* are the demons who have the oversight of nations. They would correspond to the rank of generals. *Powers* are the privates who are the demons wanting to possess human beings. The *rulers of the darkness of this world* are those demons who have charge of Satan's worldly business. *Spiritual wickedness in high places* are the demons in the heavenlies who have charge of religion.

Satan has a well-organized group, and his organization is manipulating in this world right now. The heartbreak, the heartache, the suffering, the tragedies of life are the work of Satan in the background. He is the cause of the great problems that are in the world today.

We have the enemy located and identified. That enemy is spiritual. It is Satan who heads up his demonic forces. Now we need to recognize where the battle is. I think the church has largely lost sight of the spiritual battle. We feel that if we have a lovely church building and are attracting crowds and if the finances are coming in, everything is going nicely. The financial condition of a church, however, is not where the battle is. I will grant that, if a church which has been supporting itself begins to get into debt, it is an indication that something is wrong: actually, it means the battle is being lost in the spiritual realm. There should be questions such as: Are the members of the church being built up in Christ? Is the Word of God being taught? Is there a spirit of love and cooperation among the members? Is gossip reduced to a minimum? There must not be an exercise in legalism but an exercise in right relationships among those who are the brethren in Christ. Where there is a spirit of criticism and of bitterness and of hatred, the Spirit of God cannot work.

Churches like to talk about the numbers who come to Christ. They like to talk about how many decisions they have had. Yet when the facts are really boiled down and examined and you look for the so-called converts two years later, you often find that they have disappeared. We don't seem to realize that there is a spiritual warfare being carried on today and that people need to be grounded in the Word of God. It is a manifestation of demonic power that people are being blinded and carried away into all kinds of cults and religions and "isms" with false beliefs. As a result of all this, the Word of God sinks into insignificance in such churches and organizations. This is the work of the enemy, Satan and his demonic hosts.

THE SOLDIER'S PROTECTION

Wherefore take unto you the whole armour of God, that ye may be able to withstand in the evil day, and having done all, to stand [Eph. 6:13].

We have identified the enemy. Now Paul begins to identify the arsenal which is available for defense. Nowhere is the believer urged to attack and advance. The key to this entire section is the phrase *to stand.*

The Bible speaks of believers as pilgrims. As pilgrims we are to walk through the world. The Bible speaks of us as witnesses, and we are to go to the ends of the earth. As athletes we are to run. We are to run with our eyes fixed upon the Lord Jesus Christ: ". . . and let us run with patience the race that is set before us, looking unto Jesus the author and finisher of our faith . . ." (Heb. 12:1–2). However, when the

Bible speaks of us as fighters, it says we are to stand. Very frankly, I would rather do a great deal of old-fashioned standing than fighting.

Many years ago Billy Sunday, the evangelist, attracted a great deal of attention by saying that up on the speaker's platform he was fighting the devil. I think that there was a great element of truth in that, because it was a spiritual battle. The battle is carried on wherever the Word of God is preached and the gospel is given out. That's the battle line today. That is where the enemy is working. The enemy is not working down on skid row or partying it up on Saturday night.

Years ago when I was active in Youth for Christ as a young preacher, I was out every Saturday night. We used to say at that time that Saturday night was the devil's night and we were making it the Lord's night. Well, now that I have had many more years to observe the situation, I think the devil was at home in bed. I think he was resting up so he could come to church the next morning. Why should he want to fight his own crowd? They belong to him. I'm not sure he's proud of them. In fact, I think he's ashamed of a lot of these alcoholics and these down-and-outers and these up-and-outers. He could take no pride in them. He would rather be out fighting where the spiritual battle is.

Personally, I never felt that I should carry on that battle. That is, I never felt I should make the attack. The command is to stand. It is the devil who will make the attack. Our command is, "Having done all, to stand."

I have never been enthusiastic about a group of defeated Christians singing, "Onward, Christian soldiers, marching as to war." I think it is more scriptural for the believer to sing, "Stand up, stand up for Jesus, ye soldiers of the cross." Just to be able to stand in an evil day is a victory for the believer.

This is an hour when my heart is sad as I look at a great many churches. I love the local church and the local pastors. There are a great number of wonderful pastors fighting the battle. They are the men who are really on the battlefront today. I go to so many Bible conferences as a speaker because I want to help them. I have been a pastor long enough to know how wonderful it felt and how I always appreciated it when others came to me and stood shoulder to shoulder with me. My heart is sick when I see the attendance way down and the interest gone in churches that at one time were great churches. The members were blind to the fact that a battle was being fought there, a spiritual battle.

Do you pray for your pastor on Saturday night? Don't criticize him, but rather *pray* for him. He needs your prayers. The devil gives him enough opposition. You don't need to join the crowd that crucifies the man who is preaching the Word of God. You ought to uphold his hands as Aaron and Hur upheld the hands of Moses on behalf of Israel. My heart goes out to pastors who are in need of congregations who will stand with them.

Stand therefore, having your loins girt about with truth, and having on the breastplate of righteousness;

And your feet shod with the preparation of the gospel of peace [Eph. 6:14–15].

"Stand therefore." This is the fourth time he gives this exhortation to the believer. This is the only place that I find Paul laying it on the line and speaking like a sergeant. Earlier he said, "I beseech you," but now he gives the command to stand. Not only are we to be in a standing position, but we are also to have on certain armor to protect ourselves. We are not to be outwitted by the wiles of the devil; we are to be ready for his attacks.

"Having your loins girt about with truth." In the ancient garment of that day, the girdle about the loins held in place every other part of the uniform of the soldier. It was essential. To tell you the truth, if the girdle was lost, you lost everything. The garments would fly open and the pants would fall down. We see this routine in comedies, and the people laugh to see a man trying to run or fight with his trousers drooping down. It looks funny in a comedy routine, but it is not funny in a battle. A great battle in the past, we are told, was won by a clever general who told his men to cut the belts of their enemy while they were sleeping. The next morning the enemy troops were so busy holding up their trousers that they weren't able to shoot their guns and, therefore, they lost the battle. We are told to be girded with truth in the face of the enemy. Truth is that which holds everything together. What is that truth? It is the Word of God.

We need people to give out the Word of God and to give it out just as it is written. Today we have many people giving testimonies. We have football players, baseball players, movie stars, television stars, all giving testimonies. Many of them do not know any more Bible than does a goat grazing grass on a hillside. We need people whose loins are girt about with truth. They need to *know* the Word of God. (I could give you the names of a dozen peronalities who have gone off on all sorts of tangents, into cults and "isms.") I admit that some testimonies are thrilling to hear, but they are coming from folk who are standing there about to lose all their spiritual garments! They are not girded about with truth, which is the Word of God.

Every piece of this armor really speaks of Christ. We are in Christ in the heavenlies, and we should put on Christ down here in our earthly walk. Paul has already told us to put on Christ. He is the One who is the truth, and we should put Him on in our lives.

Any testimony that does not glorify Jesus Christ should not be given. There are too many testimonies that glorify the individual, such as, "I was a great athlete," or "I was a great performer, and now I am turning over my wonderful talent to Jesus." The implication is: *Believe me, He is lucky to have me in His crowd!* Friend, you are lucky if you have *Him*. He didn't get very much when He got you, and He didn't get very much when He got me. This is a day when the little fellow really doesn't have very much to say. We get the impression that we need to be someone great in the eyes of the world. No, what we need is to have our loins girt about with truth so that we can give a testimony that glorifies Christ. Christ is the truth. Truth alone can meet error.

"Having on the breastplate of righteousness." Christ is the righteousness of the believer. I do think, however, that it includes the practical righteousness of the believer. Let's be clear that the filthy rags of self-righteousness are useless as a breastplate, but I do think that underneath there should be a heart and a conscience that is right with God. Only the righteousness of Christ can enable the believer to stand before men and before God, but the heart that is to be protected should be a heart that is not condemning the believer. It is an awful condition to have sin in the life while we are trying to carry on the battle. We can never win it that way.

"Your feet shod with the preparation of the gospel of peace." Shoes are necessary for standing. They speak of the foundation. We need a good, solid foundation, and preparation is foundational. I remember in hand-to-hand combat we were taught to make sure our feet were anchored. Are your feet anchored on the Rock? Christ is your foundation in this world. No other foundation can any man lay but the one that is laid, Jesus Christ (see 1 Cor. 3:11). We are to put on Christ. Oh, how we need Him today as we face a gainsaying world and also spiritual wickedness in the darkness of this world!

> **Above all, taking the shield of faith, wherewith ye shall be able to quench all the fiery darts of the wicked.**
>
> **And take the helmet of salvation, and the sword of the Spirit, which is the word of God:**
>
> **Praying always with all prayer and supplication in the Spirit, and watching thereunto with all perseverance and supplication for all saints [Eph. 6:16–18].**

The armor of the believer is a spiritual armor because we fight against a spiritual enemy. We are to stand in that armor, and that armor is Christ, the living Christ. Satan himself, in the Book of Job, describes how God protects His own. He said, "Hast not thou made an hedge about him, and about his house, and about all that he hath on every side? . . ." (Job 1:10). God has provided protection for us today in the armor He supplies.

"Above all, taking the shield of faith." The shield covered all of the armor. The shield referred to is a large shield the size of a door. It was the shield of the heavy infantry. A soldier stood behind it and was fully protected. Christ is both the door to salvation and the door that protects the believer from the enemy without. This is the picture in John, chapter 10. Christ is both salvation and security.

"Faith" enables us to enter the door: "I am the door: by me if any man enter in, he shall be saved, and shall go in and out, and find pasture" (John 10:9). That is salvation. What about security? Faith places us securely in His hands: "My sheep hear my voice, and I know them, and they follow me: and I give unto them eternal life; and they shall never perish, neither shall any man pluck them out of my hand" (John 10:27–28). Faith enables us to lay hold of the Lord Jesus Christ. Faith also enables us to stand behind that shield which will quench all the fiery darts of the wicked one.

"The fiery darts of the wicked." He is shooting them fast and furiously. I remember that when I was in college, I had a brilliant philosophy professor who had studied in Germany. I respected his intellect, although I didn't realize at that time he was intellectually dishonest. I looked up to him but, very frankly, he was taking my feet out from under me. I would try to answer him in class when I probably should have kept my mouth shut. But we became friends, and we used to walk together across the campus after class and discuss the questions I had raised. I came to the place where I went to the Lord in prayer and said, "Lord, if I can't believe Your Word, I don't want to go into the ministry." Then the Lord in a very miraculous way sent me to hear a man who was the most brilliant man, I think, whom I have ever heard. He gave me the answer to my questions. Then I began to learn that when a fiery dart comes my way and I don't have the answer, I am to put up the shield of faith. And this is what I have been doing ever since. I have found that the shield of faith has batted down the fiery darts of the wicked one.

I remember that I was upset about questions concerning the Genesis record of creation. I was ready to get out of the ministry because I couldn't accept certain things. The problem was not with my pygmy intellect, although I thought it was at the time; I just didn't know enough. So I put up the shield of faith.

Someone was walking with me in Israel as we were observing some excavations. He asked me, "Suppose they dig up something down there that looks like it disproves the Bible. What position would you take?" I answered, "I would put up the shield of faith, and that would bat down the fiery darts of the wicked one. I have learned that when a fiery dart is batted down, I will get the correct answer later on." I remember a time when the authorship of John was being questioned—was the Gospel of John written by John? Today it is pretty well established that John was the writer, but at one time I had questions about it.

The fiery darts of the wicked one come fast and furiously, and they are going to continue to come. The only thing that will bat them down is this shield of faith. It is like a big door. The hoplites, the heavily armed soldiers in the Greek infantry, could move with those tremendous shields, put them out in front of them, and stand protected shoulder to shoulder, while the enemy shot everything they had at them. When the enemy was out of ammunition, they would move in, certain of victory. That is the way to stand against the fiery darts of the evil one.

"And take the helmet of salvation." The helmet protects the head, and God does appeal to the mind of man. I recognize that He appeals to the heart, but God also appeals to the intellect. Throughout the Scriptures God uses reason with man. "Come now, and let us reason together, saith the LORD: though your sins be as scarlet, they shall be as white as snow; though they be red like crimson, they shall be as wool" (Isa. 1:18). "And as he reasoned of righteousness, temperance, and judgment to come, Felix trembled, and answered, Go thy way for this time; when I have a convenient season, I will call for thee" (Acts 24:25). Paul reasoned with Felix; he appealed to the mind of the man as well as to his heart. "So then faith cometh by hearing, and hearing by the word of God" (Rom. 10:17).

A theology professor who was a liberal said many years ago when I was a student, "Faith is a leap in the dark." That is not true. God does not ask you to take a leap into the dark. In fact, God says if it is a leap in the dark, don't take it. God wants you to leap into the light. God has a solid foundation for you, and how wonderful it is!

Christ is the salvation of the sinner. He is the One to receive the glory in it all. That plume on the top of the helmet is Christ. He has been made unto us salvation. "And she shall bring forth a son, and thou shalt call his name JESUS: for he shall save his people from their sins" (Matt. 1:21). Even before His birth in Bethlehem He was marked out as the Savior.

Paul mentions this helmet in connection with salvation again in another epistle. "But let us, who are of the day, be sober, putting on the breastplate of faith and love; and for an helmet, the hope of salvation" (1 Thess. 5:8).

All the parts of the armor mentioned so far have been for defense. Have you noticed that? Everything is for the front of the individual. There is no protection for his back; nothing is provided for retreat. Believe me, a retreating Christian is certainly open season for the enemy; the enemy can get through to him.

Now we have two weapons for offense. The first one is the Word of God, called the sword of the Spirit. "For the word of God is quick, and powerful, and sharper than any two-edged sword, piercing even to the dividing asunder of soul and spirit, and of the joints and marrow, and is a discerner of the thoughts and intents of the heart" (Heb. 4:12). Christ is the living Word of God. He used the Word of God to meet Satan in the hour of His temptation. Out of His mouth goeth a sharp two-edged sword in the battle of Armageddon (see Rev. 1:16; 19:21). He gains the victory with that sword. What is it? It is the Word of God. We need that sharp sword going out of our mouths today. The Word of God is a powerful weapon of offense. You and I are to use it.

Our second weapon of offense is prayer—"praying always with all prayer and supplication in the Spirit." Praying in the Holy Spirit is not turning in a grocery list to God. It means that you and I recognize our enemy and that we lay hold of God for spiritual resources. We lay hold of God for that which is spiritual that we might be filled with all the fullness of God. Paul here distinguishes between prayer and supplication. Prayer is general; supplication is specific. All effective prayer must be in the Spirit.

THE SOLDIER'S EXAMPLE—PAUL WAS A GOOD SOLDIER OF JESUS CHRIST

Here is Paul's example for us from his own experience:

And for me, that utterance may be given unto me, that I may open my mouth boldly, to make known the mystery of the gospel,

For which I am an ambassador in bonds: that therein I may speak boldly, as I ought to speak [Eph. 6:19–20].

"And for me." Paul now asks for prayer on behalf of himself. As he comes to the conclusion of this epistle, he moves into the area of the personal. He was a prisoner in Rome, and he suffered from a thorn in the flesh. Yet he does not ask for prayer that these physical handicaps be removed, but that he might proclaim courageously the mystery of the gospel.

"To make known the mystery of the gospel." The gospel is a mystery that was not revealed in the Old Testament as it is now. The New Testament reveals that Christ died for all sins, was buried, rose again on the third day. This is the gospel and the message Paul was preaching.

"I am an ambassador in bonds." Paul had just written about the spiritual warfare, and now we see that he was experiencing the onslaught of the enemy at the very moment he was writing.

"That therein I may speak boldly." Paul asks for prayer that he may speak the gospel with boldness. We need that same prayer. We need a boldness to declare the Word of God.

But that ye also may know my affairs, and how I do, Tychicus, a beloved brother and faithful minister in the Lord, shall make known to you all things:

Whom I have sent unto you for the same purpose, that ye might know our affairs, and that he might comfort your hearts [Eph. 6:21–22].

Tychicus not only carried the epistle to the Ephesian believers, but he also gave a personal account of the conditions of and the prospects for the apostle Paul. Tychicus, the pastor of the Ephesian church, is an example of the many faithful servants of Christ in the early church. The apostle Paul had great confidence in him.

"That he might comfort your hearts." Tychicus would allay any fears that the Ephesians might have about the condition of the apostle

Paul. The brotherly love exhibited in the early church is the undertone of all of Paul's epistles. Paul had a real concern for the brethren.

BENEDICTION

General Douglas MacArthur said that old soldiers do not die; they just fade away. Listen to Paul's farewell.

Peace be to the brethren, and love with faith, from God the Father and the Lord Jesus Christ.

Grace be with all them that love our Lord Jesus Christ in sincerity. Amen [Eph. 6:23–24].

Paul's own swan song is found in 2 Timothy 4:6–8: "For I am now ready to be offered, and the time of my departure is at hand. I have fought a good fight, I have finished my course, I have kept the faith: henceforth there is laid up for me a crown of righteousness, which the Lord, the righteous judge, shall give me at that day: and not to me only, but unto all them also that love his appearing." Paul reflected what a good soldier of Christ should be and what rewards awaited him.

He closes with a twofold benediction. Most of the great words of the gospel are contained in it: peace, love, faith, grace. Hope is absent, for the believer is in the heavenly places where all is realized.

"Peace" was the form of greeting of the Jewish world. A sinner must know the grace of God before he can experience the peace of God. This is the peace of God which passes all understanding.

"Love" in verse 23 means love for the other believers. This is a fruit of the Holy Spirit.

In verse 24 the "love" is of the believer for the Lord Jesus Christ, and this love is in *incorruptness* (a better translation than "in sincerity").

"Faith" means faith in Christ which produces active love. These flow from God the Father and the Lord Jesus Christ.

"Grace" is the key word of the epistle. It opened the epistle (Eph. 1:2) and is the subject of the epistle (Eph. 2:7–8). It now concludes the epistle. It is a fitting word because it is God's grace which saved us and which sustains us today.

BIBLIOGRAPHY
(Recommended for Further Study)

Bruce, F. F. *The Epistle to the Ephesians*. Westwood, New Jersey: Fleming H. Revell Co., 1961.

Foulkes, Francis. *The Epistle of Paul to the Ephesians*. Grand Rapids, Michigan: Wm. B. Eerdmans Publishing Co., 1963.

Hendriksen, William. *Exposition of Ephesians*. Grand Rapids, Michigan: Baker Book House, 1967.

Hodge, Charles. *An Exposition of Ephesians*. Grand Rapids, Michigan: Wm. B. Eerdmans Publishing Co., 1856.

Ironside, H. A. *In the Heavenlies*. Neptune, New Jersey: Loizeaux Brothers, 1937. (Especially good for young Christians)

Kelly, William. *Lectures on Ephesians*. Oak Park, Illinois: Bible Truth Publishers, n.d.

Kent, Homer A., Jr. *Ephesians: The Glory of the Church*. Chicago, Illinois: Moody Press, 1971. (An excellent, inexpensive survey)

McGee, J. Vernon. *Exploring Through Ephesians*. Pasadena, California: Thru the Bible Books, 1961.

Meyer, F. B. *Ephesians—Key Words of the Inner Life*. Fort Washington, Pennsylvania: Christian Literature Crusade, n.d. (Devotional)

Moule, Handley C. G. *Studies in Ephesians*. Grand Rapids, Michigan: Kregel Publications, 1893. (Excellent. Romans, Philippians, Colossians, and Philemon in the same series; 2 Timothy apart from this series)

Paxson, Ruth. *Wealth, Walk, and Warfare of the Christian*. Westwood, New Jersey: Fleming H. Revell Co., 1939. (Excellent devotional emphasis)

Strauss, Lehman. *Devotional Studies in Galatians and Ephesians.* Neptune, New Jersey: Loizeaux Brothers, 1957.

Vaughan, W. Curtis. *Ephesians: A Study Guide Commentary.* Grand Rapids, Michigan: Zondervan Publishing House, n.d.

Wiersbe, Warren W. *Be Rich.* Wheaton, Illinois: Victor Books, n.d.

Wuest, Kenneth S. *Ephesians and Colossians in the Greek New Testament.* Grand Rapids, Michigan: Wm. B. Eerdmans Publishing Co., 1953.